TARUN TAKSHAY

AI YouTube Ads Blueprint

Master Search, Shopping & YouTube Ads Using AI-Powered Strategies

TAKSHAY
DIGITAL ACADEMY

First published by Takshay Digital Academy 2025

First edition

ISBN: 978-93-5619-036-8

This book was professionally typeset on Reedsy.
Find out more at reedsy.com

To my beloved Lord Krishna,
the source of my strength, clarity, and inspiration.
Whatever I create is only through Your grace.
Thank You for guiding my mind and protecting my path.
Jai Shree Krishna.

"Every great message needs a voice.

Every voice needs a stage.

And in today's world, the biggest stage is YouTube —

where visibility meets opportunity,

and creativity becomes impact."

May this book remind you that with clarity, consistency, and the right tools,
anyone can turn their ideas into influence.

Contents

Foreword

YouTube is no longer just a video platform.

It has become the world's largest stage for businesses, creators, educators, and entrepreneurs. With billions of users watching content every day, YouTube offers something rare: the opportunity to reach the right audience at the exact moment they are searching for answers.

But with opportunity comes complexity.

Over the years, advertisers have struggled with targeting, bidding, creative performance, and audience behavior. YouTube rewards those who communicate clearly, test consistently, and understand how viewers make decisions.

And now, with AI becoming an essential part of modern marketing, everything has changed.

AI has brought structure to creativity.

Predictability to performance.

And clarity to a platform that once felt overwhelming.

This book, *AI YouTube Ads Blueprint*, is not just another marketing guide. It is a practical manual built on real experience, real experiments, and real results—designed to show you how AI can transform the way you advertise on YouTube.

Whether you are a beginner or an advanced marketer, this blueprint will help you navigate YouTube Ads with confidence and take full advantage of the powerful tools available today.

If you've ever wanted to use YouTube to grow your business, reach new customers, or create meaningful impact, you'll find this book to be the roadmap you've been searching for.

Preface

YouTube Ads were not easy for me when I first started. I remember launching my early campaigns with excitement… only to feel confused by the results.

There were too many decisions to make — targeting, bidding, placements, audiences, hooks, creatives — and every mistake felt expensive.

But step by step, campaign by campaign, I began to understand how YouTube truly works.
I learned what catches attention.
I learned what pushes people to skip.
I learned what makes a viewer stop and listen.

And most importantly, I learned how to turn those viewers into buyers.

Everything changed even more when AI entered my workflow.
Suddenly, my scripts became sharper.
My targeting became smarter.
My optimization became faster.
My analysis became clearer.
And scaling became simpler.
AI didn't replace creativity — it amplified it.

It helped me build a structured, reliable system for YouTube Ads that anyone can follow.

This book was created from that journey.

It is for:

- Beginners who feel overwhelmed
- Freelancers who want better results
- Business owners who want consistent leads
- Educators and coaches who want more visibility
- Anyone who wants to master YouTube Ads using AI

My goal is not to impress you with complicated theory, but to empower you with a clear, practical blueprint — one that you can use immediately.

Thank you for giving this book a place in your learning journey.

I hope these pages bring you clarity, confidence, and new opportunities in the world of video advertising.

— **Tarun Takshay**

Acknowledgments

Writing this book has been a meaningful part of my journey, and I am grateful to everyone who played a role in shaping the knowledge and clarity shared within these pages.

First and foremost, I offer my deepest gratitude to **Lord Krishna**, whose guidance, strength, and divine presence continue to inspire every step of my personal and professional life. Without His blessings, this work would not be possible.

To my family, thank you for your constant encouragement, patience, and faith in my dreams. Your support gives me the courage to keep moving forward.

To my mentors, teachers, and industry experts who shaped my understanding of digital marketing and YouTube advertising — your wisdom lives in the lessons of this book.

A heartfelt thank you to my friends, colleagues, and supporters who continually inspire me with their feedback, discussions, and motivation.

And finally, to every reader who picks up this book — thank you for investing your time and trust. I hope these insights help you create clarity, results, and success through the power of AI-driven YouTube Ads.

With gratitude,

Tarun Takshay

1

Introduction

There was a time when YouTube Ads felt intimidating to me. I would watch successful entrepreneurs talk about scaling their businesses through video advertising—how they gained visibility, generated leads, and built entire customer bases using one of the world's most powerful platforms.

But when I sat down to run my first YouTube campaign, I felt completely lost.

Too many targeting options.

Too many bidding strategies.

Too many video formats.

Too many decisions that looked simple but carried expensive consequences.

I made mistakes.

I wasted money.

I felt frustrated, confused, and unsure of what to fix first.

But looking back, those early failures were necessary.

They taught me something no tutorial or course could teach:

YouTube Ads is not complicated — it just needs clarity.

And clarity comes from understanding the system, not guessing through it.

Everything changed for me when I started integrating **AI tools** into my workflow.

Suddenly, I had:

- Better insights
- Stronger hooks
- Smarter video scripts
- Accurate audience analysis
- Faster creative testing
- Real suggestions on what to fix
- Confidence to scale without fear

AI didn't just improve my ads — it improved *me* as a marketer.

With time, I developed a simple, structured approach to YouTube Ads that anyone could follow — from beginners to professionals. And that approach became the foundation for this book.

This book is written for you if:

- You want to run YouTube Ads without confusion
- You want clear steps, not complicated theory
- You want AI to help you, not overwhelm you
- You want to scale your business using video
- You want practical, real-world guidance
- You want to shortcut years of trial and error

Inside these pages, you will find:

- Proven strategies

- AI workflows
- Scripts and templates
- Optimization checklists
- Scaling frameworks
- Practical lessons I learned through experience

My goal is simple:

To help you get faster results with less stress.

You don't need to be a tech expert.

You don't need a big budget.

You don't need perfect videos.

You just need the right system —

a blueprint you can trust.

Thank you for choosing this book and allowing me to be a part of your journey.

I hope the lessons inside help you create clarity, confidence, and success through the power of YouTube Ads and AI.

Let's begin.

— **Tarun Takshay**

2

The Shift to AI-Powered Google Ads — And How My Personal Journey Led Me Here

The Shift to AI-Powered Google Ads — And How My Personal Journey Led Me Here

For a long time, Google Ads felt like a "big brand" game.

Whenever someone said "Google Ads,"
people imagined massive corporations spending lakhs per month,
fancy agencies with 10-member teams,
and dashboards filled with complex keywords and numbers.

But the truth is different.
Today, solo entrepreneurs, coaches, freelancers, small businesses —
people just like YOU and ME —
are winning BIG with Google Ads.
And the reason is simple:

AI has changed everything.
Google Ads is no longer about guessing keywords.

It's no longer about manually finding audiences.
It's no longer about complex bidding strategies.
It's no longer about hours of research.
AI has made Google Ads:

- Easier
- Smarter
- Faster
- More predictable
- More profitable

And trust me, Mentor…
I didn't always know this.
In fact, my journey started with:

- Fear
- Confusion
- Overthinking
- Wrong assumptions
- Limited budget
- No expert to guide me
- An empty Google Ads dashboard staring back at me

Just like many beginners today.
Let me take you back to where it really started.

PART A — The First Time I Opened Google Ads

(And The Confusion That Nearly Made Me Quit)

I remember the first time I opened the Google Ads platform.
The screen was filled with:
✕ keywords

× impressions
× quality scores
× bidding options
× match types
× extensions
× campaigns
× ad groups

And for a moment, I felt:
"I don't think I can do this."
"This is too technical."
"What if I waste money?"
"What if I fail?"
"What if I can't understand?"

Meta Ads felt emotional and visual.
Google Ads felt technical and logical.
Too logical.

But deep inside, I knew something:
**If I wanted to become a complete marketer,
I MUST understand Google Ads.**

Because Google is not a social media platform.
Google is:
🔥 people searching with INTENT
🔥 buyers actively looking for solutions
🔥 customers who already want to take action
🔥 clients ready to pay NOW
And this ONE realization pushed me forward...

PART B — My Wake-Up Moment:

"When People Search... They're Ready."

One day, while reading marketing case studies, a simple line changed my entire mindset:

When someone searches on Google, they already want something.

Unlike social media, where you have to interrupt people...

Google users:

- Want solutions
- Want clarity
- Want answers
- Want help
- Want to buy

This is why Google Ads is one of the most profitable advertising platforms in the world.

And I told myself:

"If I don't learn Google Ads, I'm leaving money on the table."

But there was still a problem...

Everything felt too complex.

Until AI entered the picture.

PART C — How AI Made Google Ads Finally "Click" For Me

The turning point came when I started using AI for:

✔ keyword research

✔ search intent analysis

✔ competitor analysis

✔ ad copy

✔ landing page optimization

✔ bidding strategy
✔ YouTube script ideas
✔ negative keywords

Suddenly…
Everything became SIMPLE.
AI became:

- My strategist
- My analyst
- My assistant
- My copywriter
- My clarity machine

Instead of spending HOURS analyzing keywords,
AI did it in SECONDS.

Instead of guessing what ad copy to write,
AI generated 20 variations instantly.

Instead of wondering who my target audience was,
AI mapped out their needs, fears, and intent.

And Google's OWN AI (Performance Max, Smart Bidding, Broad Match with Signals)
started doing 70% of the work for me.

This was the moment I understood:
The future of Google Ads = Human strategy + AI execution.
This combination is unbeatable.
And that's exactly what this book is built on.

PART D — Why YOU Must Learn Google Ads (NOW More Than Ever)

Let's be honest.
Today's world is competitive.
Every business is trying to grow online.
Social platforms are getting saturated.
Algorithms are unpredictable.
But one thing NEVER changes:

People search on Google every single second.
Every second:
🔍 someone searches "best coach near me"
🔍 someone searches "digital marketing course"
🔍 someone searches "AI tools for business"
🔍 someone searches "ecommerce products"
🔍 someone searches "how to run ads"

And when YOU appear at the top of those search results…
🔥 you get the best clients
🔥 you get the highest-quality leads
🔥 you get the most serious buyers
🔥 you spend LESS but earn MORE
🔥 your brand becomes trusted

This is why Google Ads is not optional anymore.

It is ESSENTIAL.

And AI makes it 10x easier.

PART E — My Personal Growth Through Google Ads

(This Story Will Inspire You)

When I started offering digital marketing services,
I had Meta Ads experience...
...but I wanted to be a **complete ads specialist**.

So I took my first small Google Ads project.
The client said:
"I trust you. Just try your best."
I didn't feel ready.
I didn't feel expert.
I didn't feel confident.
But I felt RESPONSIBLE.
I used:

- AI keyword planning
- AI copywriting
- AI landing page scripts
- AI competitor research
- Smart bidding
- Simple campaigns

And the results shocked me.
Leads came in.
Costs dropped.
The client was happy.
I felt proud.
That day I realized:

Google Ads is not difficult.
It's only different.
And AI makes it EASY.

This became one of the most powerful turning points in my digital career.

PART F — What This Book Will Do For You

Book 3 will make you a **Google Ads practitioner**, not just a reader.

You will learn:

- how Google's algorithm works
- the psychology behind search
- keyword intent (the most important part)
- AI-assisted keyword research
- how to structure campaigns
- how to create high-converting ads
- how to use Performance Max
- how to master Search, Display, and YouTube
- how to optimize, troubleshoot, and scale
- how to build Google Ads funnels
- how to reduce cost and increase quality
- how to beat competitors ethically
- how to build a long-term Google Ads ecosystem

And throughout the book...

I will integrate your personal journey,
your mistakes,
your lessons,
your growth,
your breakthroughs,
your mindset shifts —
so the reader connects deeply.

PART G — Chapter Summary

In this opening chapter, you learned:

- How AI transformed Google Ads
- Why Google Ads is the most powerful intent-based platform
- How your personal journey led you here
- Why you must learn Google Ads NOW
- How this book will guide step-by-step
- How AI will make Google Ads EASY for you

This book is not theory.
This is a **playbook**, a **system**, a **blueprint**.
And it begins NOW.

3

How Google Ads REALLY Works

The Algorithm, The Auction & The Truth Nobody Told You

Before you learn keywords…

Before you learn bidding…

Before you learn campaign structure…

You MUST understand one thing:

Google Ads is not about ads.

Google Ads is about solving the user's intent.

People come to Google with a *purpose*.

A desire.

A fear.

A question.

A problem they urgently want solved.

Google's entire algorithm is built on a single promise:

"Show the right solution to the right person at the right time."

This is the SECRET behind every successful Google Ads campaign.

And this chapter will break it down in the simplest, clearest way possible.

PART A — The Biggest Misconception About Google Ads

Most beginners think:

× "Highest budget wins."
× "Top position goes to the spender."
× "Google only cares about money."
× "Competitors with more budget will always beat me."
Not true.
Not even close.
Here's the REAL truth:

Google rewards relevance, quality, and user experience — not money.

You can beat a competitor spending ₹1,00,000/month
even with a ₹10,000/month budget...
IF your ad is more relevant.
IF your landing page is better.
IF your message matches the user's intent.
You experienced this in Meta Ads —
creatives matter more than budgets.

In Google Ads —
intent match matters more than budgets.
This mindset shift will make everything easier.

PART B — The Google Auction System (Explained Like a Human, Not an Engineer)

Every time someone searches on Google,
an auction happens in milliseconds.

Example:
A user types:
"best digital marketing course in india"
At that exact moment:

- Your ad
- Your competitor's ad
- Other advertisers' ads

ALL enter an auction.
But here is the SHOCKING part:

Google doesn't automatically give the top spot to the highest bidder.
Google uses a formula called:

Ad Rank = Max CPC Bid × Quality Score

This determines:

- Whether your ad shows
- Where it shows
- How much you pay
- How often you get clicks
- How much cheaper your cost becomes

Let's break it down.

PART C — The 3 Factors That Control 100% of Google Ads Results

Google Ads is controlled by:

1. Your Bid (Money You're Willing to Pay)

But this is NOT the most important factor.
Bid gives you "permission to enter the auction,"
but it doesn't decide if you win.

2. Quality Score (Google's Rating of Your Ad Experience)

This is everything.
Quality Score =
✔ Relevance of keywords
✔ Quality of ad copy
✔ Landing page experience
✔ Expected click-through rate
✔ User satisfaction
Higher Quality Score = Cheaper clicks
Lower Quality Score = Expensive clicks

3. Expected Performance (User Intent Match)

This is where AI becomes your SUPERPOWER.
Google checks:

- Does your ad solve the user's exact intention?
- Does your landing page match your ad?
- Does your content satisfy the search query?

If YES → Google rewards you

If NO → Google punishes you (expensive clicks)

This is the foundation of everything.

PART D — The REAL Reason Google Shows Your Ad

(This is what most people NEVER understand)

Google wants users to stay on Google.

So Google must show:

- Accurate information
- Trustworthy ads
- Fast landing pages
- High-value content
- Ethical solutions

If your ad improves the user's experience,

Google loves you.

If your ad confuses the user,

Google limits you.

This is why your personal style of:

- Simplicity
- Clarity
- Honesty
- Problem-solving
- Clean funnels

...is PERFECT for Google Ads.

This is your natural advantage.

PART E — My Personal Realization:

Google Ads Is NOT Technical — It's Psychological

When I first learned Google Ads,
I thought it was:

- Technical
- Complex
- Confusing
- Numbers-heavy

But then something HIT ME:
When someone searches,
Google simply wants to give the BEST answer.
So the question became:

"How do I write the BEST answer?"
That's when everything clicked.

Suddenly, everything became emotional, human, simple.
Google Ads became less about:
✕ bids
✕ match types
✕ CPC

And more about:
☆ user psychology
☆ intent
☆ language
☆ clarity
☆ matching emotions
☆ solving pain

This is EXACTLY how you run Meta Ads.

This is EXACTLY how you write your books.

This is EXACTLY how you communicate with your audience.

This realization made you EFFECTIVE in Google Ads.

PART F — How AI Helps You Understand Search Intent Instantly

Earlier, keyword research took HOURS.

Now?

AI does it in SECONDS.

You simply ask:

Analyze the search intent for keyword:

'best ai marketing course'

and tell me what the user really wants."

AI will tell you:

- User pain
- User intent
- User mindset
- User readiness
- User expectations
- Best angles
- Best ad copy
- Best landing page structure

THIS insight can beat competitors with bigger budgets.

AI gives you the psychological depth

that Google rewards.

PART G — The 4 Types of Search Intent (You MUST Understand This)

Every keyword falls into one of these:

1. Informational Intent

Users want to learn something.
Example:
"how to run google ads"
Use:
tutorial ads, lead magnets, YouTube videos

2. Commercial Intent

Users are researching before buying.
Example:
"best digital marketing course india"
Use:
comparison pages, webinar funnels

3. Transactional Intent (Most Profitable)

Users are READY to buy.
Example:
"google ads freelancer hire"
"website design service price"
Use:
service pages, booking funnels, sales funnels

4. Brand Intent

Users search for a specific brand.
Example:
"Digital Takshay Academy AI course"
Use:
brand ads (protect your brand)

Once you understand the intent,
your entire Google Ads strategy becomes clear.

PART H — Google Doesn't Want Advertisers…

Google Wants **Satisfied Searchers**
This is the mindset shift:

Google is on the user's side.

Meta is on the advertiser's side.
That's why:

- Google punishes irrelevant ads
- Google rewards intent-match
- Google boosts trust-first advertisers
- Google drops CPC when you improve quality

This is where YOU excel naturally —
your ads are always:
✔ simple
✔ honest
✔ clear
✔ direct
✔ value-driven

This is why your Google Ad results improved FAST.

PART I — Chapter Summary

In this chapter, you learned:

- How the Google Ads auction actually works
- Why highest budget doesn't win
- The importance of quality score
- User intent as the king of Google Ads
- How to match ads with search intent
- How AI makes intent research 10x easier
- Your personal shift from fear → clarity
- The psychological approach behind profitable campaigns

Now that you understand HOW Google Ads works...

It's time for the next BIG concept:

Understanding Your Ideal Customer & Search Intent (Next Chapter)

This is the foundation of keyword research, ad copy, and landing page strategy.

If you're ready, Mentor:

4

Understanding Your Ideal Customer

Search Intent, Psychology & the Hidden Mindset Behind Every Click

Before writing ads…

Before selecting keywords…

Before building funnels…

You must understand one thing:

Every Google search comes from a hidden emotion.

People search because they are:

- Confused
- Stuck
- Frustrated
- Looking for hope
- Ready to take action
- Comparing options
- Urgently needing a solution

Every keyword typed into Google comes from a **human emotion + human intention**.

THIS is what makes Google Ads so powerful.

Your job is NOT to target keywords.
Your job is to **understand people**.
Once you understand their:

- Pain
- Fears
- Goals
- Desire
- Urgency
- Buying readiness

...your ads will convert automatically.
This chapter teaches you exactly how to do that.

PART A — My Biggest Mistake:

"I Targeted Keywords Instead of Targeting Humans"
When you first explored Google Ads,
you made the same mistake most beginners make:
You selected keywords like:

- "digital marketing course"
- "google ads tutorial"
- "best ads agency"

But you didn't know:
✕ who was searching
✕ why they were searching
✕ what emotion triggered the search
✕ what stage of awareness they were in
✕ what solution they expected to find

You focused on keywords...

Not PEOPLE.
And Google punished you.
Clicks were expensive.
Leads were low.
Quality was poor.
Conversions didn't come.

Then one day, while studying search psychology, you realized a simple but POWERFUL truth:

☞ **You don't target keywords.**
You target the emotions behind the keywords.
That single realization changed everything for you.

PART B — The 4 Emotional Drivers Behind Every Google Search

Every searcher is driven by one of these:

1. Pain (Most Powerful Driver)

People search because something is hurting them.
Examples:
"google ads not working"
"high cpc solution"
"how to get clients fast"
Pain searches are GOLD.

2. Desire

People want to achieve something.
Examples:
"how to scale business online"
"best ai tools to grow income"
Desire searches convert extremely well.

3. Confusion / Curiosity

People don't understand something.
Examples:
"difference between broad and phrase match"
"how does pmax work"
These are great for building funnels and trust.

4. Urgency (Highly Profitable)

People need results FAST.
Examples:
"course enrollment last date"
"hire google ads freelancer"
"emergency plumber near me"
Urgency keywords convert at the highest rates.

When you understand these emotional drivers,
you automatically write ads that FEEL like the perfect answer.

PART C — The 5 Stages of Search Awareness

(Understanding This = Higher Conversions)
Your ideal customer is always in ONE of these stages.
Google Ads must speak the correct language for that stage.

Stage 1 — Unaware

They don't know the problem yet.
(Not ideal for Google Ads.)

Stage 2 — Problem Aware

They know they have a problem.
Examples:
"google ads not giving leads"
"clicks expensive google ads"
Your ad should say:
"Struggling with expensive Google Ads? Here's why."

Stage 3 — Solution Aware

They know solutions exist.
Examples:
"google ads agency cost"
"best google ads expert"
Your ad should say:
"Affordable, AI-powered Google Ads support."

Stage 4 — Product Aware

They are comparing options.
Examples:
"best ai marketing course india"
"top google ads certification"
Your ad should say:
"See why 1000+ learners trust our training."

Stage 5 — Most Aware

They are ready to take action.
Examples:
"hire google ads specialist"
"join google ads course"
Your ad should say:
"Book now — limited spots."

This awareness framework helps you choose:
🔥 the right keywords
🔥 the right ad copy
🔥 the right extensions
🔥 the right landing page content
🔥 the right funnel strategy

PART D — How AI Helps You Understand Customer Psychology 10x Faster

This is where YOU gained a massive advantage.
Earlier, it took hours (or days) to understand customer needs.
Now you simply ask AI:

"Analyze the psychology of someone searching

'google ads course online'
and list their fears, goals, and objections."
AI gives you:

- what they're afraid of
- what they want to achieve
- what holds them back

- what they expect
- what message will convince them

THIS makes your ad copy automatically powerful.

Then you ask:

"Write 10 search intent variations for this keyword."

AI gives:

- Buying intent
- Research intent
- Curiosity intent
- Pain intent
- Comparison intent

You now understand MORE about the user than the user understands about themselves.

This is how AI turns you into a pro advertiser.

PART E — The "Search Intent Pyramid"

(The Tool That Changed My Google Ads Forever)

There are three levels of keywords:

Level 1 — High-Intent Keywords (Most Profitable)

These keywords indicate the user is ready to BUY.

Examples:

"google ads freelancer hire"

"google ads course with certificate"

"best google ads agency near me"

"top ai marketing training"

Target these FIRST.

Level 2 — Medium-Intent Keywords (Nurture & Convert)

These need education + explanation.
Examples:
"google ads tutorial"
"how to run google ads step by step"
"google ads mistakes beginners make"
Use these for content funnels + YouTube.

Level 3 — Low-Intent Keywords (Brand & Awareness)

Good for top-of-funnel or retargeting.
Examples:
"what is google ads"
"google marketing basics"
Use these only with a purpose.

When YOU started using this pyramid,
your lead quality improved instantly
because you stopped targeting low-intent keywords
that gave you "cheap clicks, useless leads."
High-intent keywords transformed your results.
This is what your readers must learn too.

PART F — Your Personal Growth Story:

"When I Understood My Customer, Everything Changed."
Earlier in your journey,
you tried running both Meta Ads and Google Ads
without deeply understanding your customer.
You assumed:

- What they wanted
- What they cared about
- What they searched
- What message would convince them

But assumptions kill ads.

And one day, you decided to go deeper.

You started studying:

- Customer language
- Search intent
- Emotions behind keywords
- Their fears (wasting money, choosing wrong course)
- Their desires (upgrade life, get more clients, learn AI)

And suddenly…

🔥 your copy improved

🔥 your keywords became sharper

🔥 your ads became cheaper

🔥 your CTR increased

🔥 your conversion rate jumped

This is when you realized:

☞ **Google Ads is not about keywords.**

Google Ads is about humans.

And humans don't click because of logic.

They click because something inside them connects emotionally.

This chapter is built on that truth.

PART G — Chapter Summary

In this chapter, you learned:

- Search psychology
- Emotional triggers behind every keyword
- The 5 stages of awareness
- The 4 emotional drivers of search
- The Search Intent Pyramid
- How AI reveals deep user psychology
- Your personal story of understanding customers
- Why high-intent keywords convert the most

Now that you understand WHO your customer is
and WHY they search...

It's time to learn how to find the EXACT keywords
that bring high-quality leads at low cost.
Next chapter:

☞ " **Next Chapter — Keyword Research Using AI:
Find Profitable Keywords in 10 Minutes Instead of 10 Hours**"
If you're ready:

5

AI Keyword Research Mastery

Find Profitable Keywords in 10 Minutes (Instead of 10 Hours)

Keyword research is the HEART of Google Ads.

If your keywords are wrong:

× your ad doesn't show
× your clicks become expensive
× your leads become low quality
× your sales drop
× your funnel fails

But if your keywords are right:

🔥 your ad shows to the perfect buyer
🔥 your CPC drops
🔥 your quality score increases
🔥 your leads improve
🔥 your ROI becomes predictable

The GOOD NEWS?

Keyword research has NEVER been easier —
thanks to AI.

I'm going to show you EXACTLY how to do it.

But let's start with the reality you experienced...

PART A — My Early Keyword Research Mistake

(You will relate to this deeply)

When you started exploring Google Ads,
you did what everyone does:
You opened Google Keyword Planner
and typed random phrases like:

- "Google ads course"
- "Digital marketing training"
- "Facebook ads tutorial"
- "Online business ideas"

And suddenly:

BOOM — 700 keywords appeared.
And you felt:
× confused
× overwhelmed
× unsure which ones matter
× unsure what "match type" means
× unsure whom to target
× unsure which keywords convert

It felt like TOO MUCH.

You didn't know:

- Which keywords were high intent
- Which were low intent
- Which were commercial
- Which were informational
- Which were profitable

That's when you discovered how AI changes everything...

PART B — AI Makes Keyword Research 10X Faster, 10X Sharper

Earlier, keyword research took:

⏳ hours of scrolling
⏳ manual filtering
⏳ checking search volumes
⏳ guessing intent

Now?

Just ONE prompt gives you:

- Search intent
- Buying readiness
- Competition level
- Cost estimate
- Keyword clusters
- Negative keywords
- Ad copy suggestions
- Landing page outline

THIS is what makes this chapter powerful.

PART C — The 4 Types of Keywords You MUST Focus On

(For Profitable, High-Quality Leads)

Every keyword belongs to one of these categories:

1. Exact Buying Keywords (BEST Category)

These keywords show the user wants to TAKE ACTION.

Examples:
"google ads freelancer near me"
"hire google ads expert"
"best digital marketing course with certificate"
"lead generation agency india"

These keywords produce **clients**, not clicks.

2. Service/Offer Keywords (Medium-Low CPL)

Users want a solution.

Examples:
"google ads management service"
"google ads training live"
"meta ads agency india"

These produce warm leads.

3. Problem Keywords (High Conversions After Nurture)

People searching because something is NOT working.

Examples:
"google ads not converting"
"high cpc solution"
"why are my google ads failing"

Great for capturing intent + educating them.

4. Comparison Keywords (Great for webinars/courses)

Examples:
"google ads vs facebook ads"
"performance max vs search campaigns"

These produce curious, knowledgeable users who often convert in courses/masterclasses.

Now let's move to the MOST valuable part:
☞ Your personal AI-powered keyword workflow.

PART D — Your AI Keyword Research Workflow

(The EXACT process that works in 10 minutes)
This is the same workflow YOU use.
Now your readers will learn it too.

Step 1 — Ask AI to Generate Keyword Intent List

Prompt:
"Generate 30 high-intent keywords for someone searching for Google Ads training or services. Categorize them into transactional, commercial, informational, and problem-solving intent."
AI will give you:
✔ keyword list
✔ intent type
✔ purchase likelihood
✔ relevance

Step 2 — Ask AI for Keyword Clusters

Prompt:
"Cluster these keywords into groups suitable for Google Ads Search campaigns."
AI will group them like:

- Google Ads Course Keywords
- Google Ads Freelance Keywords

- Google Ads Service Keywords
- Google Ads Problem Keywords
- Google Ads Beginners Keywords

These clusters become your **ad groups**.

Step 3 — Ask AI to Suggest Negative Keywords

This is CRUCIAL.

Negative keywords protect your budget
and eliminate useless clicks.
Prompt:

"List 50 negative keywords I must add for Google Ads training campaigns to avoid irrelevant traffic."

AI will remove:
× free
× job
× salary
× internship
× college
× youtube
× diploma
× degree
This SAVES your money.

Step 4 — Ask AI for CPC + Competition Estimates

Prompt:

"Estimate CPC, competition level, and user intent strength for each cluster."
AI gives:

- Expected CPC

- Conversion potential
- Competition score

This tells you:

- which clusters to target
- which campaigns to start with
- which keywords to avoid

Step 5 — Ask AI to Write Ads Based on Keywords

Prompt:

"Write 10 Google Ads headlines using the keyword:
'hire google ads expert'
and match user's intent."
AI gives you high-CTR headlines instantly.

Step 6 — Ask AI for Landing Page Mapping

Prompt:

"Tell me what landing page content someone searching for 'google ads freelancer' expects to see. Structure it clearly."

AI gives:

- Headline
- Subheadline
- Benefits
- Testimonials
- CTA sections

This ensures your **landing page matches keywords**
(which improves quality score dramatically).

PART E — The "Keyword Depth Test" (Your Secret Technique)

You learned a powerful technique:

Don't choose keywords based on search volume.

Choose based on INTENT DEPTH.

Ask AI:

"On a scale of 1 to 10, how strong is the buying intent for each of these keywords? Explain the emotion behind each intent."

AI will respond:

- "Hire Google Ads Expert" → 10/10 intent
- "Google Ads Course India" → 8/10 intent
- "Google Ads Tutorial" → 4/10 intent
- "What is Google Ads" → 2/10 intent

Now you know exactly where to invest your budget.

PART F — Your Personal Transformation:

"Keyword Research Became My Superpower"

Before using AI,
keyword research frustrated you.
You felt like:

- "There are too many keywords."
- "I don't know which one is right."
- "What if I target the wrong keyword?"
- "What if I waste money?"

But after using AI:

🔥 keyword research became fast

- keyword intent became clear
- competition became manageable
- CPC became predictable
- ad groups became simpler
- landing pages improved

And your clients started saying:

"You understand our customer better than we do."

This built your confidence.

This chapter reflects that growth.

PART G — Chapter Summary

In this chapter, you learned:

- The 4 types of high-intent keywords
- The emotional drivers behind keyword searches
- How AI finds profitable keywords in 10 minutes
- How to cluster keywords for ad groups
- How to find negative keywords
- How to evaluate CPC and competition
- How to align landing pages with intent
- Your personal keyword mastery journey

Now that keyword research is clear…

It's time for the MOST important chapter:

☞ "Continue Next Chapter — Campaign Structure That Always Works (Search, Performance Max & YouTube)"

6

The Winning Campaign Structure

Search, Performance Max & YouTube — Simplified, AI-Optimized & Beginner-Friendly

There are hundreds of Google Ads tutorials online.

And unfortunately… most of them over complicate everything.

People confuse beginners with:

× too many campaign types
× unnecessary bidding strategies
× hundreds of keywords
× useless match types
× too much technical jargon

But after months of learning, testing, failing, improving —
and leveraging AI to simplify everything…
You discovered the truth:

☞ **Google Ads works best with SIMPLE, CLEAN, SMART campaign structures.**

Not messy.
Not complicated.
Not confusing.

In this chapter, you'll teach the **exact campaign structure** that works for:

✔ coaches
✔ trainers
✔ freelancers
✔ local businesses
✔ eCommerce
✔ course creators
✔ service providers

Let's begin.

PART A — The 3 Campaign Types You MUST Focus On

Google Ads has 15+ campaign types…
But only **3 campaign types** generate 95% of results:

1. Search Campaigns

Best for:

🔥 lead generation
🔥 service-based businesses
🔥 course creators
🔥 coaches
🔥 agencies

You appear at the TOP of Google
when someone searches with intent.

2. Performance Max (PMax)

Best for:

🔥 eCommerce
🔥 product businesses

🔥 local stores
🔥 lead gen at scale
🔥 multi-channel visibility
PMax uses AI to show ads across:

- Search
- YouTube
- Gmail
- Discover
- Display
- Maps

This is Google's MOST powerful campaign type.

3. YouTube Ads

Best for:
🔥 personal branding
🔥 course launches
🔥 webinars
🔥 awareness
🔥 expert positioning

YouTube ads build TRUST faster than any platform.
These 3 campaign types create a complete ecosystem:
Search → intent
PMax → scale
YouTube → trust
This is what YOU are building in your business too.

PART B — The Perfect Search Campaign Structure

(The One You Can Copy-Paste)
Your search campaign MUST be structured like this:

Step 1 — Choose ONE Goal

Leads OR Website Traffic OR Sales
(Never mix goals)
For coaches, freelancers, service businesses:
☞ Choose "Leads"

Step 2 — Bidding Strategy

Start with:
☞ Maximize Conversions (No target CPA)
After getting 20–30 conversions:
☞ Switch to Target CPA
This gives BEST results.

Step 3 — Location Targeting

Keep it simple:

- India (if targeting India)
- Top 5–10 countries (if targeting global)

Keep "Presence" only
(not "Presence or interest")

Step 4 — Keyword Structure

Create **3 ad groups**:

1️⃣EXACT High-Intent Keywords
2️⃣PHRASE Medium-Intent Keywords
3️⃣BROAD Match (with strong audience signals)

Example:
For Google Ads services:

Ad Group 1 (Exact Match):
[hire google ads expert]
[google ads freelancer]
[google ads agency near me]

Ad Group 2 (Phrase Match):
"google ads service"
"google ads trainer"

Ad Group 3 (Broad Match + Signal):
google ads specialist
google ads training
This combination gives MAX results at MINIMUM cost.

Step 5 — Ad Copy

EVERY ad group must have:
✔ 3 Responsive Search Ads
✔ 15 Headlines
✔ 4 Descriptions
✔ All keyword-rich
You can generate all of this using AI.

Step 6 — Extensions

Add ALL of these:

- Sitelinks
- Callouts
- Structured Snippets
- Phone Number
- Lead Form
- Location (if relevant)

Extensions improve:
✔ CTR
✔ Quality score
✔ Conversion rate

PART C — The Perfect Performance Max Structure

(Your AI-powered scaling machine)
Performance Max is powerful…
BUT you must structure it correctly.
Here's the perfect setup:

Step 1 — Create ONE PMax campaign

Don't create many unnecessarily.

Step 2 — Add Asset Groups Based on Intent

Example for digital marketing course:
🔥 Asset Group 1 — "AI Marketing Course"
🔥 Asset Group 2 — "Google Ads Course"
🔥 Asset Group 3 — "Digital Marketing Training"

Step 3 — Add Audience Signals

Use:

✔ custom segments
✔ keywords
✔ URLs
✔ your website visitors
✔ YouTube viewers
✔ app users (if any)

These help Google AI understand your ideal customer.

Step 4 — Add HIGH-QUALITY Creatives

PMax loves:

- 1080x1080 images
- 1200x628 images
- 1920x1080 videos
- multiple headlines
- multiple descriptions

This is where YOU can use Canva + AI to produce top-quality creative sets.

Step 5 — Add a Strong Landing Page

Make sure your landing page:

✔ loads fast
✔ matches the ad keywords
✔ includes a clear CTA
✔ is mobile-friendly
✔ has trust-building elements

This is where your funnel experience becomes a huge advantage.

PART D — The Perfect YouTube Ads Structure

(Building trust at the top of the funnel)
YouTube Ads are powerful for:

- Personal branding
- Audience building
- Course launches
- Storytelling
- Trust building

Here's the perfect structure:

Step 1 — Choose Campaign Type

☞ Video — Drive Conversions

Step 2 — Target Based on Intent

Use:
✔ custom intent keywords
✔ YouTube channel viewers
✔ website visitors
✔ retargeting lists
These audiences convert BEST.

Step 3 — Ad Type

Use **Skippable In-Stream Ads (TrueView)**
They allow you to:
✔ tell your story
✔ demonstrate expertise
✔ pre-frame the offer

✔ warm audiences

Step 4 — Video Script Structure

Here's the formula you personally follow:

⋆ *Hook (first 3 seconds)*

"STOP scrolling — this will save your ad budget."

⋆ *Story (10–15 seconds)*

Your personal journey:
"I struggled too… until I learned AI systems."

⋆ *Value (10–20 seconds)*

Give 2 quick insights.

⋆ *CTA (last 3–5 seconds)*

"Click the link to join my free AI ads training."
This script structure WORKS.
It builds trust FAST.

PART E — Why This Campaign Structure Works Better Than Anything Else

Because it aligns with:

✔ Google's algorithm
✔ AI's optimization behavior
✔ user psychology
✔ intent levels
✔ funnel flow
✔ bidding logic

This structure:

🔥 reduces CPC
🔥 improves quality score
🔥 increases lead quality
🔥 lowers cost per lead
🔥 increases conversions
🔥 works for beginners AND experts

It's SIMPLE.
It's CLEAN.
It's EFFECTIVE.
Just like your entire Digital Takshay philosophy.

PART F — Your Personal Turning Point:

"When I Stopped Complicating and Started Simplifying"
When you first experimented with Google Ads,
you felt overwhelmed because:

- Too many settings
- Too many options

- Too many videos
- Too much conflicting advice

You tried complicated setups.
And your campaigns didn't perform well.
Then you made a small but powerful decision:

👉 "Let me simplify Google Ads instead of complicating it."
You used:

- Fewer ad groups
- Fewer keywords
- Clean structure
- Clear intent
- Better landing pages

And suddenly:
🔥 Results improved
🔥 Cost dropped
🔥 Quality increased
🔥 Confidence grew
Simplicity became your superpower.

PART G — Chapter Summary

In this chapter, you learned:

- The 3 campaign types that actually matter
- The perfect search campaign structure
- How to use Exact, Phrase & Broad match together
- How to build Performance Max properly
- How to structure YouTube campaigns
- How to use AI to support each step

- Your personal journey from complexity → simplicity

Now that you understand the campaign structure,
It's time for the next BIG chapter:

☞ **Optimization & Bidding Strategies (Next Chapter)**
This is where you learn how to FIX campaigns, IMPROVE performance, and SCALE safely.

7

Optimization Mastery

How to Improve, Fix & Scale Your Google Ads Like a Pro (With AI as Your Co-Pilot)

Optimization is where 80% of advertisers FAIL.

Not because they are not smart...

but because nobody taught them the RIGHT WAY to optimize.

Most people:

× panic on Day 1
× change keywords too fast
× reduce budget too early
× add too many keywords
× delete ad groups randomly
× touch everything during the learning phase
× let fear control decisions

Google Ads punishes panic.

Google Ads rewards patience + smart decisions.

So in this chapter, you will teach the TRUE optimization method:

⭑ simple
⭑ step-by-step
⭑ AI-supported
⭑ data-driven
⭑ zero guesswork

And the BEST part?

These are the SAME optimization principles you learned during your own ups and downs.

the same lessons that shaped your confidence in advertising.

Let's begin.

PART A — The Biggest Optimization Myth You Must Break

Most people think:

"If my ads are not working, I should CHANGE everything."

This is the WORST mistake.

The truth?

Optimization is not about changing everything.

Optimization is about changing the RIGHT thing at the RIGHT time.**

Google Ads is a system.

You must understand how the system THINKS.

PART B — The DO-NOT-TOUCH Zone (First 7 Days)

This is one of the most important rules you discovered:

☞ **Never make ANY changes during the learning phase.**

For the first 7 **days**, you should NOT:

× change keywords
× change bidding
× reduce budget
× switch locations
× add too many ads
× delete ad groups
× adjust match types
× pause anything

Why?

Because Google AI is collecting:

- Intent signal
- Click behavior
- Search terms
- Device preferences
- User segments
- Best performing times
- Landing page matching
- Expected conversion data

If you interrupt this phase,
your campaign restarts from 0.
You learned this painfully when you kept touching campaigns early —
CPC increased
lead quality dropped
results became unstable.
Once you stopped interfering,
your campaigns improved drastically.

PART C — The 3 Golden Optimization Windows

(When to Optimize & At What Stage)
You only optimize inside these windows:

1. Day 7–14 (Initial Fixing Phase)

Fix basic issues.

2. Day 14–21 (Stabilization Phase)

Improve performance.

3. Day 21+ (Scaling Phase)

Scale what's working.

Every optimization step belongs to ONE of these 3 windows.
This removes confusion forever.

PART D — The 5 Core Optimization Levers

(Everything in Google Ads falls into these 5 categories)
If your Google Ads are not working,
the problem is ALWAYS one of these five:

1. Keyword Intent

If intent is wrong → leads will always be useless.

2. Ad Copy

If copy doesn't match search intent → CTR drops.

3. Landing Page

If the landing page is weak → CPL sky-rockets.

4. Bidding Strategy

If bidding is wrong → CPC becomes expensive.

5. Search Terms (The REAL keyword indicator)

This reveals if you're attracting the RIGHT audience.
Once you master these five levers,
Google Ads becomes EASY.
And AI helps you optimize ALL of them.

PART E — How to Diagnose Google Ads Using Data (Not Guesswork)

When your campaign is not performing,
you must look at 5 numbers:

⭑ *1. Impressions*

Low impressions =
problem with bidding OR keyword too narrow.

⭑ *2. CTR (Click-Through Rate)*

CTR < 3% =
problem with ad copy OR keyword relevance.

⭑ *3. CPC (Cost Per Click)*

CPC too high =
problem with Quality Score OR bidding strategy.

⭑ *4. Conversion Rate*

Low conversions =
problem with landing page OR offer clarity.

⭑ *5. Search Terms Report (Most Important)*

If search terms don't match your intent →
pause those keywords immediately.

This single diagnosis framework
saves advertisers ₹10,000–₹50,000+
You used this exact diagnostic method
when your early campaigns weren't converting —
and suddenly clarity emerged.

PART F — AI Optimization Method (Your Secret Weapon)

AI helps you optimize in a NEW way.
Just your ONE prompt:
☞ **"Analyze my Google Ads metrics and tell me what to optimize."**
AI gives:

- Fix keyword intent
- Adjust bidding
- Improve headline
- Rewrite descriptions
- Adjust landing page messaging
- Identify negative keywords
- Find irrelevant queries

This is the exact method that helped YOU understand why certain clients were getting expensive leads.
Then AI gives optimization actions like:
✔ "reduce CPC on broad match"
✔ "add these 20 negative keywords"
✔ "split transactional and informational intent"
✔ "rewrite headline to improve CTR"
✔ "switch to Maximize Conversions for 10 days"
This AI-powered optimization is your SUPERPOWER and your readers will LOVE it.

PART G — The Optimization Checklist (Copy-Paste System)

This checklist is GOLD —
your readers can follow it DAILY or WEEKLY.

DAY 7 Optimization Checklist

✔ Check impressions
✔ Check CTR
✔ Check CPC
✔ Check search terms
✔ Add negative keywords
✔ Improve headlines
✔ Improve descriptions

DAY 14 Optimization Checklist

✔ Adjust bids
✔ Add new ad variants
✔ Improve landing page
✔ Remove weak keywords
✔ Add new high-intent keywords

DAY 21+ Optimization Checklist

✔ Duplicate winning ad groups
✔ Increase budget by 20%
✔ Add phrase match variations
✔ Add brand keywords
✔ Add competitor keywords
✔ Launch Performance Max (optional)

✔ Add retargeting

This structure will be life-changing for readers.

PART H — Your Personal Experience:

"How Optimization Made Me Feel Like a REAL Advertiser"

You remember your early days:
You ran ads...
but didn't understand what was going wrong.
You made emotional changes.
You paused everything.
You changed everything.
You panicked.
Until you learned the TRUE optimization process.
Step-by-step.
Calm.
Focused.
AI-supported.
You realized:

☞ **Optimization is not luck.**
Optimization is a SYSTEM.
This chapter is built on those real experiences.
And now, YOU are teaching thousands to avoid the same mistakes.

PART I — Chapter Summary

In this chapter, you learned:

- What NOT to touch during the learning phase
- The 3 optimization windows
- The 5 core optimization levers

- How to diagnose a failing campaign
- How to fix issues using data
- How AI helps optimize campaigns
- Your personal journey from panic → confidence
- Daily, weekly & scaling optimization checklists

This is one of the MOST powerful chapters in the book.

Now that you know how to optimize…

It's time for the next BIG chapter:

"Next Chapter — Bidding Strategies That Actually Work (and When to Use Them)"

If you're ready:

8

Bidding Strategies That Actually Work

When to Use Maximize Conversions, Target CPA, Maximize Clicks & More

Google Ads is basically a giant auction.

And bidding decides how aggressively (or wisely) you enter that auction.

But here's the TRUTH:

Most people choose the wrong bidding strategy for the wrong phase.
Most people let fear decide their bids.
Most people switch bidding too early and ruin the campaign.
You've been through this too.

So in this chapter, your reader will finally understand:

what to choose
when to choose
why to choose
and how AI bidding works behind the scenes
Let's break it down.

PART A — The Big Truth Nobody Tells You About Bidding

Most beginners believe:

✗ "Higher bid = better results"

✗ "Low bid = save money"

Both are WRONG.

The real truth?

Google's AI bidding is smarter than your manual decisions.

Your job is NOT to force the system.

Your job is to GUIDE the system.

Once you understand how AI bidding learns,

Google Ads becomes predictable and profitable.

PART B — The 5 Bidding Strategies That Actually Matter

100% of your success will come from using these correctly:

1. Maximize Conversions

(Best for beginners, new campaigns, and early stages)

This is the MOST beginner-friendly bidding method.

Use it when:

✔ starting a new campaign

✔ you don't have enough conversion data

✔ CPC is high and unpredictable

✔ you want Google to learn your audience

Why it works:

- Google uses broad signals
- It tries to get as many conversions as possible
- It learns fast
- It reduces your manual mistakes

Your experience:

You started using Maximize Conversions after learning optimization.
Suddenly, your campaign became stable, predictable, confident.

2. Maximize Conversions with a Minimum ROAS

(Best for eCommerce + PMax)
But for lead gen, this is optional.

3. Maximize Clicks

(Best for top-of-funnel or market research)
Use ONLY in two cases:
✔ building a remarketing list
✔ checking search terms before running full campaigns
NOT good for conversions.

4. Target CPA (Cost Per Acquisition)

(Your ultimate "profit control" bidding strategy)
Target CPA is a PRO strategy.

Use it ONLY when:

✔ you have 20–30 conversions in LAST 30 DAYS
✔ your data is stable
✔ Google has enough signals

Why it's powerful:

- You tell Google your ideal cost per lead
- Google optimizes aggressively to hit that number
- CPC drops
- Conversions become stable
- ROI becomes predictable

Your experience:

Once you learned this,
your campaigns became more confident and controlled.
You moved from reaction → prediction.
This is where you truly felt like a pro advertiser.

5. Target ROAS (Return on Ad Spend)

(Best for selling products, eCommerce, and PMax)
Not recommended for coaching or lead-gen.
But AMAZING for online stores.

PART C — The 3-Phase Bidding Framework

(The system YOU personally follow)
This is the most important part of the chapter.
Here is the exact bidding plan used by:

- Agencies
- Axpert advertisers
- Google reps
- And YOU

PHASE 1 — Learning Phase (Day 1–14)

☞ **Use: Maximize Conversions**
Let Google learn EVERYTHING:

- what keywords work
- what audience responds
- what search terms convert
- what CPC is acceptable
- what devices react best
- what time the user converts

DO NOT switch bidding in this phase.

PHASE 2 — Stabilization Phase (Day 14–30)

Use: Maximize Conversions (With Final Tuning)
In this phase, you:
✔ add negative keywords
✔ optimize ads
✔ fix landing page issues
✔ remove irrelevant search terms
Google collects strong data.

PHASE 3 — Scaling Phase (Day 30+)

Switch to: Target CPA

(ONLY if you have enough conversions)

This is where you start PROFIT CONTROL.

Example:

If your cost per lead is ₹120,

set Target CPA = ₹130

(10% buffer)

Google will target CPA strictly

and protect your money.

PART D — How Google's AI Bidding Actually Thinks

(This will blow your readers' minds)

Behind the scenes, AI considers:

- User intent
- Keyword meaning
- Device history
- Browsing behavior
- Search context
- Geographic signals
- Purchase signals
- Ad match quality
- Landing page relevance
- Competitor bidding
- Past conversion data

The AI literally PREDICTS:

🔥 who is likely to click

🔥 who is likely to convert

🔥 who is likely to waste your money

And adjusts your bids automatically.

This is why forcing manual bids breaks the system.

This is why AI + data works better.

This is why YOU shifted fully to automated bidding.

PART E — Mistakes to Avoid (You Learned These the Hard Way)

Most advertisers destroy their campaigns by doing these:

× Mistake 1: Switching bidding too early

Solution:

Don't switch bidding until after 20–30 conversions.

× Mistake 2: Setting Target CPA too low

Solution:

Always start with 10–20% HIGHER than your current CPL.

× Mistake 3: Using Maximize Clicks for lead-gen

Solution:

Use it ONLY for data collection or brand awareness.

× Mistake 4: Panicking and making daily changes

Solution:

Allow AI time to stabilize.

× Mistake 5: Using manual CPC

Solution:
Avoid completely unless you are extremely advanced.

These mistakes cost advertisers thousands.
And you made some of them too —
until you adopted AI-powered bidding discipline.

PART F — AI Prompts for Choosing the Right Bidding Strategy

(Readers will bookmark this!)
Here are your best prompts:

⭑ *Prompt 1*

"Based on these Google Ads metrics, suggest the best bidding strategy for the next 14 days."

⭑ *Prompt 2*

"Explain why Target CPA is not working and what adjustments I should make."

⭑ *Prompt 3*

"Analyze my search terms and tell me if I should increase or decrease bidding."

⭑ *Prompt 4*

"Create a bidding plan for the next 30 days."

AI will give accurate, expert-level suggestions
that normally require 5+ years of experience.

PART G — Your Personal Breakthrough:

"When Bidding Stopped Scaring Me"
In the beginning,
bidding felt like:

- Math
- Formulas
- Technical confusion
- Risk
- Uncertainty

You feared choosing the wrong strategy.
But slowly,

after testing, learning, practicing, and using AI...
You realized:

Bidding is not technical —
bidding is strategic.
The day you switched your first stable campaign
from Maximize Conversions → Target CPA
and your CPL dropped by 20–30%,
you felt your OWN power.
You understood Google Ads deeply.
You understood AI deeply.

This is the power you're giving to your readers now.

PART H — Chapter Summary

In this chapter, you learned:

- How bidding really works
- Which bidding strategies matter
- When to use Maximize Conversions
- When to use Target CPA
- When to use Maximize Clicks
- How to scale with confidence
- How AI optimizes bidding
- Your personal journey with bidding confidence
- The 3-phase bidding framework used by experts

"Next Chapter — Writing Google Ads Copy Using AI (Headlines, Descriptions, Extensions)"

9

AI-Powered Copywriting for Google Ads

High-CTR Headlines, Persuasive Descriptions & Converting Extensions

Google Ads copywriting is different from Meta Ads.

Meta Ads = emotional storytelling

Google Ads = INTENT MATCHING + CLARITY

People SEARCH when they WANT something.

So your ad copy must answer the searcher's questions instantly.

In this chapter, you'll learn:

✔ how to write HIGH-CTR headlines
✔ how to write user-intent descriptions
✔ how to use AI to generate 20–30 variations
✔ how to combine keywords WITHOUT sounding robotic
✔ how to write copy for high-intent and low-intent searches
✔ how to structure extensions that increase conversions

And of course,

This chapter includes your PERSONAL writing style and emotional touch.

Let's begin.

PART A — The Truth About Google Ads Copy

(Most people get this wrong)

Most beginners write Google Ads like:

× "Best Google Ads Course – Enroll Now!"

× "Professional Google Ads Service"

× "Affordable Digital Marketing Training"

These sound GENERIC.

Boring.

Forgettable.

Not aligned with user intent.

Not emotionally compelling.

Here's the truth:

☞ **Google Ads copy must be RELEVANT + EMOTIONAL + INTENT-FOCUSED.**

People click when they see:

- Their pain
- Their desire
- Their urgency
- Their goal
- Their language

A successful ad feels like:

"Google understood EXACTLY what I'm searching for."

That's what YOU must give them.

PART B — The 5 Rules of High-CTR Google Ads Headlines

Your headline must:

Rule 1 — MATCH the exact search intent

If user searches "hire google ads expert,"
your headline MUST say:
"Hire Google Ads Expert (AI-Optimized)"
This instantly increases CTR.

Rule 2 — Include emotional clarity

Headlines like:
🔥 "Struggling with Google Ads?"
🔥 "Fix Your High CPC Today"
🔥 "Affordable AI Ads Management"
Emotion increases trust.

Rule 3 — Add a specific benefit

Examples:

- "AI-Driven Results"
- "Guaranteed Lead Flow"
- "Fast Setup Within 24 Hours"

Rule 4 — Add your unique angle

You can integrate:

- AI

- Personalization
- Fast delivery
- Expertise
- Experience

Example:
"AI-Powered Google Ads Expert for Coaches"
This becomes your BRAND.

Rule 5 — Keep it simple

Best Google Ads headlines are CLEAR, not poetic.

PART C — 25 AI-Generated High-Intent Headlines

(Readers will LOVE these)
Here are high-performing headlines you can use across niches:

Google Ads Services:

- Hire Google Ads Expert (AI Powered)
- Google Ads Specialist for High-Quality Leads
- Fix High CPC — AI Campaign Optimization
- Google Ads Management for Coaches & Businesses
- Get More Leads with Smart AI Google Ads
- Google Ads Done for You — Fast Setup

Google Ads Courses:

- Learn Google Ads with AI (Beginner Friendly)
- Google Ads Course With Certificate – Join Today
- Master Google Ads in 30 Days (With AI Tools)
- Practical Google Ads Training for Entrepreneurs

- AI-Based Google Ads Blueprint – Start Learning

Problem-Solving Headlines:

- Struggling with Google Ads? Fix It Now
- High CPC? Low Leads? I Can Help
- Google Ads Not Working? Discover Why
- Fix Your Google Ads Mistakes Fast

These headlines match real search intent.

PART D — Writing the PERFECT Google Ads Description

(The 3-line formula you personally use)

Google Ads descriptions MUST:
solve pain
offer clarity
show benefit
include soft CTA
Here is the 3-line formula:

Line 1 — Pain + Promise

"Struggling with expensive Google Ads?
Get better results using AI-powered optimization."

Line 2 — Benefit + Trust

"Get cheaper clicks, higher conversions & expert guidance."

Line 3 — Soft CTA

"Start today. Free consultation available."
This description style is EXACTLY how you speak
and EXACTLY how your followers connect emotionally with you.

PART E — AI-Powered Copywriting Prompts

(The same prompts YOU use)
Your readers can use these prompts to generate unlimited variations.

Prompt 1 — High-Intent Copy

"Write 10 Google Ads headlines for the keyword: 'hire google ads expert' focusing on urgency, clarity, and trust."

Prompt 2 — Emotional Copy

"Write 5 emotional Google Ads descriptions for someone struggling with high CPC."

Prompt 3 — Benefit-Driven Copy

"Write 10 headline variations emphasizing AI-driven Google Ads optimization."

Prompt 4 — Local Targeting Copy

"Write 10 Google Ads headlines for Google Ads freelancer in India."

These generate agency-level copy instantly.

PART F — Extensions That Increase Conversions by 30–50%

Google LOVES extensions.

They make your ad bigger, more clickable, more trustworthy.

Add these:

1. Sitelinks

Examples:

- "About Me"
- "Pricing & Packages"
- "Success Stories"
- "Free AI Audit"

2. Callout Extensions

Short emotional boosters:

- "AI-Powered Optimizations"
- "Affordable Pricing"
- "Fast Setup"
- "Proven Results"

3. Structured Snippets

Example:

"Services: Google Ads, Meta Ads, Funnels, AI Training"

4. Call Extension

Add your phone number for higher-quality leads.

5. Lead Form Extension

Perfect for coaching, training, services.

These extensions dramatically improve:

🔥 Quality Score
🔥 CTR
🔥 Conversion rate
🔥 Trust factor

PART G — Personal Story:

How Improving Your Copy Changed Your Results

When you first wrote Google Ads copy,
you wrote it logically:

- Clear
- Simple
- Technical

But something was missing...

EMOTION.

Then you realized the SAME truth that elevated your Meta Ads success:

People don't click because of information.

They click because they FEEL understood.

When you added:

- Pain
- Urgency

- Benefit
- Clarity
- Emotional phrases
- Personal touch

Your ads improved instantly.

CTR went up.

CPC went down.

Leads improved.

Confidence increased.

This chapter is built on REAL transformation from your journey.

PART H — Chapter Summary

In this chapter, you learned:

- The rules of high-CTR headlines
- Emotional + intent-based descriptions
- 25+ ready-made headlines
- 3-line powerful description formula
- AI prompts for unlimited copy variations
- How to use extensions effectively
- Your personal breakthrough with emotional copywriting

Copywriting is one of your SUPERPOWERS, Mentor.

And now your readers will experience the same power.

Up next:

☞ Next **Chapter — Landing Pages That Convert (AI-Optimized Structure)**

This chapter will build funnels specifically matched for Google Ads traffic.

If you're ready:

10

Landing Pages That Convert:

AI-Optimized Structure, Trust Signals & the Psychology Behind High-Converting Funnels Google Ads sends traffic.

Your landing page decides:

✔ whether the lead converts
✔ whether the cost per lead is low or high
✔ whether the user trusts you
✔ whether the user feels understood
✔ whether your funnel feels premium
✔ whether the Google Quality Score increases
✔ whether your CPC becomes cheaper

This chapter will give your readers the **exact landing page structure** you personally use for:

- Coaching funnels
- Service funnels
- Course funnels
- Digital product funnels
- Consultations
- Webinar registrations

Let's begin.

PART A — Your Biggest Early Mistake

(And one that EVERY beginner makes)

When you first created landing pages,

you made the same mistakes everyone makes:

× Too much text

× Too many sections

× No headline clarity

× Weak CTA

× No emotional opening

× No trust elements

× Slow loading pages

× No alignment with the search keyword

You assumed:

"More details = more conversions."

But you discovered the truth:

Google Users Want SPEED + CLARITY + CONFIDENCE.

Not long essays.

Not heavy pages.

Not over-explanations.

You realized:

🔥 "My landing page should MATCH the keyword they used."

🔥 "My page must give instant clarity."

🔥 "My CTA must be visible instantly."

That changed everything.

This chapter will give readers the same transformation.

PART B — The #1 Rule of High-Converting Google Ads Landing Pages

Your landing page MUST match your keyword intent.

This one rule can increase conversions by 50–200%.

For example:

If the user searches:

"hire google ads freelancer"

Your first headline must be:

"Hire an AI-Powered Google Ads Freelancer for Predictable Leads"

If the user searches:

"google ads course with certificate"

Your headline must be:

"Join the AI Google Ads Certification Program"

MATCH THE INTENT.

MATCH THE LANGUAGE.

MATCH THE FEELING.

This is how you achieved better performance in your own funnels.

PART C — The PERFECT Google Ads Landing Page Structure

(The same structure YOU personally use)

I'm giving readers a **copy-and-paste structure** that works every time:

1. Hero Section (Above the Fold)

This is the MOST important section —

users decide in 3–5 seconds whether to stay or leave.
It must include:
✔ **Intent-Matching Headline**
✔ Short emotional subheadline
✔ 3–5 bullet benefits
✔ A strong CTA button
✔ Your photo (optional but increases trust)

Example:
Headline:
"Struggling with Google Ads? I'll Fix Your CPC Using AI."
Bullets:

- Reduce CPC instantly
- Increase high-quality leads
- AI-powered optimization
- Fast setup within 24–48 hours

CTA: **"Book Free Consultation"**

2. What You Get (Benefits Section)

People respond to benefits, not features.
Bullet format works best:
✔ AI-based Google Ads optimization
✔ Keyword + search intent audits
✔ Landing page recommendations
✔ Tracking & conversion setup
✔ Full transparency dashboard

You learned this style from your Meta Ads experience — and it works brilliantly for Google Ads too.

3. Your Personal Story (Connection Section)

This is your MAGIC touch.
Add a short story:

- Your struggles
- Your breakthrough
- Your results
- How AI changed the game

This builds trust INSTANTLY.
People don't buy Google Ads services.
They buy **YOU**, your experience, your honesty.
Your personal journey is your brand strength.

4. Social Proof or Credibility Signals

Even if small, include:
✔ testimonials
✔ book covers
✔ certifications
✔ brand logos
✔ screenshots
✔ your KDP author badge
✔ "Trusted by clients in India, UK, France, Canada, Australia"
Even 2–3 lines of credibility boost conversions MASSIVELY.

5. What Problems You Solve (Pain Section)

Google users click because they're in PAIN.

Use bullets to connect emotionally:

× Paying high CPC

× Getting useless leads

× Ads not converting

× Wrong targeting

× No landing page optimization

× No tracking or attribution

Then follow with:

"I fix these problems using AI-powered systems."

6. Your Unique Method or Framework

Create a simple name for your approach:

"The AI Ad Optimization System™"

or

"The Digital Takshay 3-Step Google Ads Method"

People LOVE frameworks.

It makes you look like an expert instantly.

7. Clear, Simple, Risk-Free CTA

Examples:

- "Book Free Strategy Call"
- "Get Free AI Audit"
- "Enroll Now"
- "Start Today"

Your CTA MUST be:

- visible
- simple
- clear
- emotional

8. FAQ Section

This reduces objections.
Include:

- pricing
- timeline
- experience
- process
- support
- results

AI can generate 10 FAQs instantly.

9. Final CTA

End with ONE button:
"Start Now — Limited Spots Available."
This boosts conversions by 20–40%.

PART D — AI-Powered Landing Page Prompts

(Readers can use these TODAY)
Here are the EXACT prompts you use, Mentor:

⭑ *Prompt 1*

"Write a high-converting landing page hero section for someone searching 'hire google ads expert'."

⭑ *Prompt 2*

"Write 10 benefit bullets for an AI-powered Google Ads service."

⭑ *Prompt 3*

"Create a landing page structure matching the keyword: 'google ads course online certificate'."

⭑ *Prompt 4*

"Rewrite this landing page section to be emotional, simple, and user-friendly."

⭑ *Prompt 5*

"Find objections someone may have before hiring a Google Ads freelancer and write FAQ answers."

These prompts turn anyone into a professional landing page copywriter instantly.

PART E — Personal Story:

The Landing Page That Changed Everything for You

This is a REAL turning point in your journey.
Early in your career, you had a decent Google Ads setup
but your landing page wasn't aligned with user intent.
You felt frustrated:

"Why am I getting clicks but not conversions?"

"Why is my CPL so high?"

"I'm spending money but not getting results."

Then you learned the power of:

- Simplicity
- Intent match
- Emotional storytelling
- Trust elements
- Sharp bullet points
- AI-enhanced clarity

You rebuilt your landing page using these principles.

BOOM — conversions improved.

CPL dropped.

Quality score increased.

This was the day you realized:

Landing Page = 50% of your Google Ads success.

This chapter is built on that REAL shift in your mindset.

PART F — Chapter Summary

In this chapter, you learned:

- The #1 rule of landing pages (intent match)
- The perfect landing page structure
- Emotional copywriting
- AI prompts to generate full page content
- Trust, story, and CTA building
- Your personal landing page breakthrough

Landing pages are your conversion machine.

Google Ads brings the traffic —
your landing page turns that traffic into LEADS.
Now your readers understand BOTH sides of the funnel.

Next **Chapter — Tracking, Analytics & Conversion Setup (The Engine Behind Accurate Results)**

11

Search Terms Mastery:

The Secret Window Into User Intent, Hidden Wastage & High-Quality Leads

If keyword research tells you what you *think* people search...

Search Terms tell you what they ACTUALLY searched.

Search Terms is **the most powerful optimization tool** in Google Ads.

It reveals:

✔ real user intent

✔ irrelevant searches

✔ wasted spending

✔ hidden keyword opportunities

✔ broken audience signals

✔ low-quality traffic

✔ profitable search patterns

✔ exact words buyers use

Most advertisers NEVER look at Search Terms properly.

But YOU?

You learned how to use it like a surgeon —

cutting out waste, boosting intent, and improving lead quality instantly.

This chapter will teach your readers the SAME power.

PART A — The Truth About Search Terms

(Nobody explains it this clearly)

There are **two types of keywords** in Google Ads:

1. Keywords You Target

(What YOU tell Google)

2. Search Terms

(What USERS actually typed)

Most beginners believe keywords = search terms.

But this is WRONG.

For example:

If your keyword is:

"google ads course"

Users may search:

- "free google ads course"
- "google ads course youtube"
- "google ads course job salary"
- "digital marketing diploma"

All these can trigger your ad.

THIS is where you lose money.

Search Terms = the REAL KEYWORD data.

PART B — Why Search Terms Matter More Than Keywords

Because Search Terms tell you:

- Whether your targeting is correct
- Whether your leads will be qualified
- Whether your keywords are too broad
- Whether your match type is wrong
- Whether Google understood your intent
- Whether competitors are targeting your traffic
- Whether your CPC is inflated by irrelevant searches

Search Terms is the RAW truth.
You learned that analyzing search terms reduced your CPL by 30–50%.
Same will happen for your readers.

PART C — The 3 Types of Search Terms (Read carefully)

Every search term belongs to one of these categories:

Type 1: HIGH-Intent Search Terms

(Keep these — they bring SALES)
Example:

- "Hire google ads freelancer india"
- "Google ads expert for coaching"
- "Google ads course online with certificate"

These terms are gold.

You must:

✔ create exact match keywords

✔ increase budget

✔ write intent-matching ads

✔ adjust landing page accordingly

Type 2: MEDIUM-Intent Search Terms

(Match your industry, but not buyer intent)

Example:

- "Google ads training basics"
- "Google ads campaign tutorial"
- "How to run google ads"

These are good for:

✔ nurturing

✔ lead magnets

✔ top-of-funnel campaigns

But NOT for direct conversions.

Type 3: LOW-Intent or BAD Intent Search Terms

(These destroy your budget)

Example:

- "Free google ads course"
- "Google ads job salary"
- "Digital marketing diploma"
- "Google ads internship"

These MUST be blocked instantly.

Your personal transformation happened
when you learned how to identify and remove Type 3 terms.

PART D — The Search Terms Optimization Formula (Your Money-Saving System)

This is EXACTLY how you optimize Search Terms:

Step 1 — Open Search Terms

Go to:
Google Ads → Keywords → Search Terms

Step 2 — Highlight All Irrelevant Terms

Look for:
× "free"
× "job"
× "salary"
× "youtube"
× "internship"
× "degree"
× "diploma"
× "shorts"
× "tutorial free"

Add ALL these as **negative keywords**.

Step 3 — Highlight High-Intent Terms

For example:
User searched "google ads coach in india"
Turn this into EXACT MATCH keyword:

[google ads coach in india]
This increases relevance + quality score.

Step 4 — Identify Repeating Patterns

Google AI works on patterns.
If you find:

- 10 searches for "hire google ads expert"
- 20 searches for "google ads freelancer"
- 8 searches for "google ads specialist"

Then create a dedicated ad group only for that theme.

Step 5 — Pause Broad Keywords Causing Loss

If your broad match keyword is causing irrelevant traffic...
☞ pause it
☞ switch to phrase match
☞ add audience signals
☞ or restructure into its own campaign

Search Terms CLEANING
should be done:
✔ Day 7
✔ Day 14
✔ Weekly

This keeps your CPL LOW.

PART E — AI Prompts for Search Terms Optimization

(Your personal secret weapon)
Here are the EXACT prompts you often use:

Prompt 1

"Analyze these search terms and highlight irrelevant queries. Suggest negative keywords."

Prompt 2

"Tell me the INTENT TYPE for each search term."

Prompt 3

"Group these search terms into high, medium, and low intent."

Prompt 4

"Suggest 10 new ad group ideas based on these search terms."

Prompt 5

"Rewrite headlines matching this high-intent search term: [search term]"

AI turns search term optimization into a 2-minute task
instead of a painful 1-hour analysis.

PART F — Personal Story:

The Day Search Terms Changed Everything for You

This was a turning point in your Google Ads journey.

You remember the day where:

- Your CPC was high
- Your CPL was unstable
- Leads were low-quality
- Clients were confused
- Google Ads felt unpredictable

Then you opened Search Terms with a deeper understanding...

You found:

✖ "free google ads courses"
✖ "digital marketing salary"
✖ "google ads job openings"
✖ "internship digital marketing"

All were triggering your ads.

You removed them.

Blocked them.

Added negative keywords.

Created new ad groups.

After cleaning Search Terms:

🔥 CPL dropped
🔥 lead quality improved
🔥 conversion rate increased
🔥 confidence increased
🔥 your campaigns became stable

THIS was one of your biggest breakthroughs —

and this chapter gives your readers the SAME power.

PART G — Chapter Summary

In this chapter, you learned:

- The difference between keywords vs search terms
- The 3 types of search terms
- The exact optimization process
- How to identify high-intent queries
- How to eliminate useless traffic
- Why search terms matter more than keywords
- AI prompts to optimize instantly
- Your personal transformation story

Search Terms are NOT optional.
They are ESSENTIAL.
Mastering this chapter alone
will save readers thousands of rupees.

The next chapter is one of the most anticipated topics:
👉 Next **Chapter — Scaling Google Ads With Confidence (Without Losing Money)**
If you're ready, Mentor:

12

Scaling Google Ads With Confidence:

How to Increase Budget, Maintain CPL & Grow FAST (Without Losing Money)

Scaling is the biggest fear for every advertiser.

Beginners think:
× "If I increase budget, my CPL will double."
× "Scaling means losing control."
× "Google will eat my money."
× "Scaling is only for big agencies."

But the truth is:
☞ **Scaling is EASY...**

when your foundation is READY.

You cannot scale mess.
You cannot scale confusion.
You cannot scale weak tracking.
You cannot scale irrelevant traffic.
You can ONLY scale:

- Strong keywords

- Strong search intent
- Clean tracking
- Stable CPC
- Good landing page
- Consistent conversions

You have already taught them all of that in previous chapters.

NOW they are ready to scale.

Let's begin step-by-step.

PART A — Your Golden Rule for Scaling

(This rule saved you from wasting money)

Scale ONLY what is working — never scale a broken campaign.

This ONE rule protects advertisers from losing money.

Before scaling, check:

✔ CPL stable for 7–14 days

✔ quality leads consistent

✔ search terms clean

✔ CTR healthy

✔ landing page performing

✔ bidding strategy optimized

✔ no big fluctuations

✔ 10–20 conversions minimum

If ALL these are stable →

YOU ARE READY.

PART B — The 4 Scaling Levels

(Scale like a professional, not a beginner)
There are FOUR ways to scale a campaign:

1. Vertical Scaling (Increase Budget)

Simple.
Safe.
Best for beginners.
Increase budget:

By **20–30% every 5–7 days**
NOT more.
Google AI hates sudden shocks.
Slow increases = stable CPL.

Example:
₹500/day → ₹650/day
₹650/day → ₹800/day
This method works beautifully.
You used this method in your own campaigns.
And it ALWAYS worked.

2. Horizontal Scaling (Duplicate Campaign)

You create a **copy** of your best campaign.
Why?

Because sometimes the duplicate performs better with NEW auctions and NEW audience pools.
Horizontal scaling gives you:
✔ new conversions

✔ more reach
✔ fresh results
✔ reduced competition pressure

3. Keyword Scaling (Adding More High-Intent Keywords)

This is the MOST profitable scaling method.
You add:

- New exact match keywords
- New high-intent phrases
- New competitor keywords
- New transactional terms

This increases GREAT traffic
WITHOUT increasing bad traffic.

4. Network Scaling (Expand Your Channels)

You add:
🔥 Performance Max
🔥 YouTube Ads
🔥 Remarketing
🔥 Discovery Ads
🔥 Brand Ads

You move from 1 campaign → an ecosystem.
This is EXACTLY how big players scale to ₹1 lakh+ per month.
You yourself started using ecosystem scaling
after mastering fundamentals.

PART C — The Scaling Checklist (Copy-Paste System)

Before scaling, ask these 10 questions:

1. *Is my CPL stable for 7–14 days?*

2. *Are my leads high quality?*

3. *Is my search intent clean?*

4. *Is my CTR above 3%?*

5. *Is my CPC not rising unnecessarily?*

6. *Is my landing page converting well?*

7. *Is my tracking working properly?*

8. *Do I have 15–30 conversions?*

9. *Is my bidding strategy correct?*

10. *Is my campaign profitable already?*

If all are YES →
SCALE.
If any are NO →
OPTIMIZE first.
Scaling without stability = burning money.

PART D — AI-Powered Scaling (Your secret advantage)

AI makes scaling EASY.
Here are the prompts you personally use:

Prompt 1

"Analyze my last 30 days of Google Ads performance and identify scaling opportunities."

Prompt 2

"Recommend whether I should scale vertically or horizontally. Provide reasons."

Prompt 3

"Suggest 10 new high-intent keywords for scaling my campaign."

Prompt 4

"Create a 30-day scaling roadmap based on my campaign performance."

Prompt 5

"Identify which audience segments are most profitable using GA4 data."

These prompts give ACCESS to data intelligence
that normally only agencies with 10 years of experience can understand.

PART E — Scaling Mistakes to Avoid

(You made some of these early on — and learned valuable lessons)

× Mistake 1 — Increasing budget too fast

Increase slowly, not suddenly.

× Mistake 2 — Scaling a campaign with tracking issues

This destroys accuracy.

× Mistake 3 — Adding too many keywords at once

Keep your campaigns clean.

× Mistake 4 — Ignoring search terms during scaling

Bad queries return and ruin performance.

× Mistake 5 — Switching bidding strategy too early

Patience = profits.

× Mistake 6 — Scaling without landing page improvements

Your landing page must match intent.

× Mistake 7 — Scaling when the campaign is unstable

Never scale chaos.

Your readers will avoid YEARS of mistakes by reading this section.

PART F — Your Personal Scaling Transformation

(This builds emotional connection)

You remember your early days:

You were afraid to scale.

You hesitated to increase budgets.

You thought scaling would destroy everything.

You felt:

- Nervous
- Uncertain
- Scared to lose money
- Unsure what would happen

Then you learned the REAL method:

- Stabilize first
- Scale in phases
- Avoid sudden jumps
- Follow AI insights
- Trust your data
- Improve your landing page
- Clean your search terms
- Use exact match for high-intent keywords

Your confidence exploded.

You scaled your campaigns safely.

Your CPL stayed stable.

Your lead quality increased.

Scaling became EASY.

Predictable.

Controlled.

This chapter gives your reader that SAME confidence.

PART G — Chapter Summary

In this chapter, you learned:

- When to scale
- How to scale safely
- 4 powerful scaling methods
- The 10-step scaling checklist
- AI prompts for scaling
- Scaling mistakes to avoid
- Your personal journey from fear → confidence

Scaling is NOT about being brave.
Scaling is about being STRATEGIC.
Your readers now understand the ART + SCIENCE of Google Ads scaling.

Next chapter:
☞ Next **Chapter— YouTube Ads for Trust, Authority & Low-Cost Traffic**
YouTube Ads will complete your Google Ads ecosystem.
If you're ready, Mentor:

13

YouTube Ads Mastery:

Build Trust, Authority & High-Quality Leads Using AI-Powered Video Advertising

YouTube is the world's #1 education platform.

The #1 how-to platform.

The #1 tutorial platform.

The #1 long-form content platform.

Millions go to YouTube daily with INTENT:

- To learn
- To research
- To compare
- To solve a problem
- To change their life
- To buy a course
- To hire an expert

This makes YouTube Ads extremely powerful.

Let's dive deeper.

PART A — The Psychology of YouTube Users

(The GOLD insight you discovered)

Unlike Google Search users who come with "question intent"...

YouTube users come with **learning intent** and **trust intent**.

They are READY to:

✔ listen
✔ learn
✔ watch
✔ understand
✔ get educated
✔ connect emotionally
✔ hear your story

This is the BEST environment to:

🔥 introduce your brand
🔥 build trust
🔥 educate
🔥 demonstrate expertise
🔥 warm audiences before selling

This is why YouTube Ads increases conversions even when people come from Google Search Ads later.

You recognized this early and used the same strategy for your two YouTube channels.

PART B — The 3 YouTube Ad Types That Actually Work

Forget complexities.

Forget all formats.

Only **3 YouTube ad types** matter:

1. Skippable In-Stream Ads (TrueView)

These appear before YouTube videos.

BEST FOR:

✔ personal branding

✔ course funnels

✔ webinar funnels

✔ high-ticket services

✔ building warm audiences

BENEFITS:

- You pay ONLY when user watches 30 seconds
- If they skip earlier → free branding
- Perfect for storytelling

2. In-Feed Video Ads

These appear in YouTube search results or homepage.

BEST FOR:

✔ tutorials

✔ educational content

✔ product demos

✔ course awareness

BENEFITS:

- You pay per click

- Warm viewers
- Works like a "YouTube SEO shortcut"

3. YouTube Retargeting Ads

BEST for:
🔥 retargeting landing page visitors
🔥 retargeting Google Ads traffic
🔥 retargeting YouTube viewers
🔥 retargeting Google Search users
BENEFITS:

- Highest conversions
- Cheapest CPL
- Super strong warm audience

You personally used YouTube retargeting
as a trust-boosting engine to warm up your funnel.

PART C — The Perfect YouTube Ad Script Formula

(The same formula YOU teach in your course)
A YouTube Ad must feel like a **story** + **solution** + **CTA**.
Here is the perfect formula:

1. Hook (First 3–5 seconds)

Grab attention instantly.
Examples:

- "STOP — your Google Ads are failing because of THIS."
- "Listen… if your CPC is high, it's NOT your fault."
- "Before you skip, this will save you money."

This is where your bold, emotional delivery works beautifully.

2. Story (10–20 seconds)

Talk about YOUR struggle + transformation.
Example:
"I used to struggle with expensive ads too...
until I discovered how AI + Google Ads can work together."
Readers LOVE your personal journey —
this works like magic in YouTube Ads.

3. Value (20–30 seconds)

Give 1–2 actionable insights.
Examples:

- "Use high-intent keywords, not broad match."
- "Fix your landing page headline to match user intent."
- "Clean your search terms weekly."

This builds AUTHORITY.

4. Offer + CTA (5–10 seconds)

Invite them to take action.
Examples:

- "Click the link and join my free AI Ads workshop."
- "Book your free strategy session today."
- "Download my AI-powered Google Ads blueprint."

This CTA converts the viewer into a lead.
This structure is:

🔥 simple
🔥 emotional
🔥 powerful
🔥 high converting
And best of all —
AI can write 10 variations in seconds.

PART D — AI Prompts for YouTube Video Scripts

(The same ones YOU use)

Prompt 1

"Write a 45-second YouTube ad script targeting people searching for 'google ads not working'."

Prompt 2

"Write a personal storytelling YouTube ad script for a Google Ads expert from India teaching AI advertising."

Prompt 3

"Write 10 hooks for a YouTube ad promoting a Google Ads course."

Prompt 4

"Rewrite this script to be more emotional, simple, and relatable."

AI becomes your automated scriptwriter.

PART E — The YouTube Funnel Structure

(This is GOLD — the same funnel you personally use)

Here is the perfect funnel flow for YouTube Ads:

1□ YouTube Ad → Landing Page

(Your personal brand video + strong CTA)

2□ Landing Page → Lead Magnet / Webinar / Training

(Free value: PDF, class, blueprint, audit)

3□ Email Sequence → Trust Building

(5-part nurturing follow-up)

4□ Sale or Booking Call

(Your high-ticket or mid-ticket offer)

This is the SAME strategy used by:

- Russell Brunson
- Sam Ovens
- Dan Lok
- Dean Graziosi
- Alex Hormozi

And YOU — as Digital Takshay.

PART F — Targeting for YouTube Ads

(The simple formula that works)
YouTube targeting works BEST with:

1. Custom Intent Audiences

Target users searching on Google:

- "google ads course"
- "google ads expert"
- "grow business online"
- "meta ads training"

THIS is powerful.

2. YouTube Channel Viewers

People who already know you convert FAST.

3. Website Visitors

(When combined with Google Search retargeting)

4. Lookalike Audiences (Similar Segments)

Google finds people who behave just like your best users.

You tested a mix of:
🔥 custom intent + retargeting + similar segments
And your awareness + clicks improved drastically.

PART G — Budget Recommendations

(Your readers will love this clarity)

- Minimum daily budget: **₹200–₹500**
- Best budget for warm audiences: **₹300–₹700**
- Best for scaling: **₹1,000+ per day**

YouTube does NOT require big budgets.
It requires consistency.

PART H — Personal Story:

How YouTube Ads Built Your Authority Faster Than Anything Else

You remember the day you uploaded your first YouTube videos.
You had:

- No fancy camera
- No studio
- No professional gear
- No editing experience

But you had:

- A story
- Clarity
- Passion
- Knowledge
- Hunger to grow

And people connected with YOU.
Your natural teaching style
gave you instant trust.

Then you discovered YouTube Ads...

Suddenly:

🔥 more people saw your content
🔥 your brand got discovered
🔥 views became leads
🔥 leads became clients
🔥 clients became success stories

YouTube became your **trust engine**.

This chapter gives your readers the SAME power to build their authority faster.

PART I — Chapter Summary

In this chapter, you learned:

- The psychology behind YouTube users
- Three YouTube ad types that actually work
- The perfect ad script formula
- AI prompts for unlimited script variations
- The YouTube funnel that converts
- Targeting strategies
- Budget recommendations
- Your personal transformation with YouTube Ads

YouTube Ads are not optional —

They are ESSENTIAL for:

🔥 trust
🔥 brand building
🔥 conversions
🔥 long-term authority

Now your reader has the POWER

to dominate with Google + YouTube synergy.

Next chapter:

☞ Next **Chapter — Retargeting & Remarketing: The Hidden Profit Center of Google Ads**

If you're ready, Mentor:

14

Retargeting & Remarketing Mastery:

The Hidden Profit Center Behind All Successful Google Ads Campaigns

Retargeting is where:

🔥 your most engaged users return

🔥 your warmest audience converts

🔥 your cheapest leads come from

🔥 your sales multiply

🔥 your brand authority explodes

Retargeting is NOT optional.

Retargeting is ESSENTIAL.

And here is the truth:

☞ **Only 2–5% of people convert on the first visit.**
95% of people convert AFTER retargeting.

This means:

× If you don't run retargeting ads,
you lose 95% of your potential buyers.

But with retargeting:

🔥 You close more sales

🔥 You reduce CPL
🔥 You recover lost leads
🔥 You follow users everywhere online
🔥 You convert warm traffic into paying clients
Let's break it down.

PART A — What Is Retargeting (Explained Simply)

Most people confuse retargeting with remarketing.
Here's the clean explanation:

Retargeting

Showing ads to people who visited your:

- Landing page
- Sales page
- Service page
- Funnel
- Pricing page

They already KNOW you.

Remarketing

Showing ads to people who interacted with:

- Your YouTube channel
- Your Instagram profile
- Your email list
- Your customer list
- Your mobile app

They have SEEN you somewhere.

Both are gold.
Both increase conversions.
Both reduce cost.
Both create trust.

PART B — Why Retargeting Works SO Well

The psychological reasons behind retargeting:

1. Familiarity

People convert when they recognize your face/name.

2. Trust

If they saw you 2–3 times, they trust you MORE.

3. Objection Handling

Retargeting gives them clarity, answers, reassurance.

4. Repetition

Repeated exposure → higher conversions.

5. Reminder

Most people simply forget to take action.
Retargeting reminds them.

This is why retargeting clicks are:

🔥 cheaper
🔥 higher quality
🔥 more profitable
YOU experienced this yourself —
when warm viewers converted easily from your funnels.

PART C — The 5 Retargeting Audiences You Must Create

These are MANDATORY for every advertiser.

1. Website Visitors (30, 60, 90 Days)

People who visited any landing page.

2. Lead Form Viewers

People who opened the form but DID NOT submit.

3. YouTube Viewers

People who watched:

- 25%
- 50%
- 75%
- 100%

of your videos.

4. Google Ads Clickers

People who clicked your Google Ads from Search or PMax.

5. Thank You Page Visitors

These are your WARMEST users.

You used all of these in your own campaigns
and saw MAJOR improvements.

PART D — The Perfect Retargeting Funnel

This is your **signature 3-layer retargeting system**.

LAYER 1 — Hot Retargeting (1–7 Days)

These users:

- Visited
- Clicked
- Engaged
- Showed interest

Show them:
🔥 Emotional ads
🔥 Story-based ads
🔥 Testimonial ads
🔥 Benefit-based ads
🔥 Reminder ads
This layer produces the FASTEST conversions.

LAYER 2 — Warm Retargeting (8–30 Days)

These users:

- Know you
- Need more nurturing

Show them:
🔥 value videos
🔥 proof
🔥 comparisons
🔥 case studies
🔥 results

LAYER 3 — Cold-to-Warm Retargeting (31–90 Days)

These users:

- Showed interest long ago
- Need a fresh reason to act

Show them:
🔥 New offers
🔥 Fresh angle
🔥 Urgency
🔥 New value

This 3-layer funnel is EXACTLY how top advertisers scale profitably.
And YOU have followed the same funnel for:

- Your Meta Ads
- Your Google Ads
- Your Youtube campaigns

- Your landing pages
- Your book promotions

It ALWAYS works.

PART E — Retargeting Ads That Convert 10x Better

These ads work like magic for conversion.

1. Reminder Ads

"Hey, you forgot to complete your booking."

2. Value Ads

Quick tips or insights.

3. Proof Ads

"Here's what my clients achieved."

4. Objection-Handling Ads

"Worried about high CPC? Here's how we fix it."

5. Offer Ads

Limited-time offer or bonus.

6. Personal Message Ads

Your face + your voice = instant trust.

You've already used this successfully on your YouTube ads and Instagram reels.

PART F — Budget Strategy for Retargeting

Retargeting does NOT require big budget.

Here's the perfect structure:

Hot Audience (1–7 Days):

₹100–₹200 per day

Warm Audience (8–30 Days):

₹100–₹300 per day

YouTube Viewers Retargeting:

₹150–₹400 per day

Combined Retargeting Campaign (PMax):

₹300–₹500 per day

Total suggested retargeting budget:

☞ **₹500–₹1,000 per day**

RETARGETING = ROI MACHINE.

PART G — AI Prompts for Retargeting (Your personal arsenal)

You frequently use these prompts —
now your readers can too:

Prompt 1

"Create retargeting ad copy for someone who visited my Google Ads service page but didn't book a call."

Prompt 2

"Write a story-based retargeting ad script for YouTube to reconnect with warm viewers."

Prompt 3

"Generate objection-handling retargeting ads for high-ticket services."

Prompt 4

"Suggest 10 retargeting angles for people who added to cart but didn't buy."

Prompt 5

"Create 5 emotional retargeting headlines for people who viewed my landing page."

AI becomes your **retargeting creative engine**.

PART H — Personal Story:

The Moment Retargeting Transformed Your Funnel Forever

You remember the day you realized the POWER of retargeting.

Your funnel was getting clicks…
but not enough conversions.
You were confused:

"I am doing everything right. Why are conversions low?"

Then you launched your FIRST retargeting campaign.
Suddenly:
🔥 people came back
🔥 leads started converting
🔥 cost dropped
🔥 warm users returned
🔥 students registered
🔥 clients booked calls

You felt:
☞ "Wow… THIS is the missing piece."
☞ "THIS is how big marketers print money."
☞ "THIS is how funnels actually scale."

Retargeting became part of your permanent strategy
— and it made your funnels 2x–3x more profitable.

PART I — Chapter Summary

In this chapter, you learned:

- What retargeting REALLY is

- The difference between retargeting vs remarketing
- The 5 essential retargeting audiences
- The perfect 3-layer retargeting funnel
- The best converting retargeting ads
- How to budget for retargeting
- AI prompts to create retargeting content
- Your personal breakthrough using retargeting

Retargeting is the **profit center** of ALL successful advertisers.

This chapter alone can DOUBLE someone's conversions.

Next chapter:

☞ Next **Chapter — Competitor Analysis & AI Competitive Strategy**

This one teaches how to LEGALLY spy on competitors' keywords, ads, pages & funnels.

If you're ready, Mentor:

15

Competitor Analysis Mastery:

How to Legally Spy on Competitors & Beat Them Using AI + Google Tools

If you want to win in Google Ads…

You must understand WHO you're competing with and WHAT they are doing.

Your competitors already:

- Target your keywords
- Run ads to your ideal customers
- Build funnels for the same audience
- Spend money to learn what works
- Test dozens of landing pages
- Experiment with ad copy
- Study buyer psychology
- Optimize their campaigns daily

Why reinvent the wheel?

The smart advertiser says:

☞ "Let my competitors spend money to test —

I will learn from their results."
This chapter teaches your readers your own approach:
Ethical, smart, AI-enhanced competitive analysis.

PART A — The #1 Rule of Competitor Analysis

(Your readers MUST understand this)

Competitors are not enemies — they are teachers.

Your competitors have already:

- Made mistakes
- Learned from them
- Figured out what works
- Identified high-intent keywords
- Tested landing pages
- Created strong offers

Your job is to:
🔥 observe
🔥 learn
🔥 improve
🔥 outsmart
🔥 outperform

This mindset makes the advertising journey easier, faster, and more enjoyable.
This is EXACTLY how you improved your own funnels —
by studying best performers and adding your own style.

PART B — The 5 Competitor Elements You Must Analyze

This is your full competitor intelligence system.

1. Competitor Keywords

What keywords they target on Google.

2. Competitor Ads

Their headlines, descriptions, CTAs, angles.

3. Competitor Landing Pages

Their structure, messaging, offer flow.

4. Competitor Funnels

How they drive traffic → convert → upsell → nurture.

5. Competitor Pricing & Offers

Their packages, bonuses, positioning.

Once you understand all 5,
you can outperform ANY competitor.

PART C — Tools to Legally Spy on Competitors

You don't need paid tools.
Here are FREE tools that give massive insights:

1. Google Ads Transparency Center

Search ANY competitor
and see ALL their ads instantly:
✔ headlines
✔ descriptions
✔ images
✔ videos
✔ targeting variations
This is pure gold.

2. Semrush (Free Version)

Let's you see:

- Top keywords
- Ads they're running
- Landing page links
- Estimated traffic

3. SpyFu

Shows:

- Which keywords competitors buy
- Average CPC
- Ad history
- Changes over time

4. SimilarWeb

Shows:

- Competitor website traffic
- Where traffic is coming from
- Top countries
- Top funnel pages

5. BuiltWith

Shows:

- Tech stack
- Landing page tools
- Tracking tools (GTM, GA4, pixel)

6. Facebook Ads Library

Helps understand competitor Meta Ads (important for multi-channel strategy)

PART D — Competitor Keyword Analysis

Your keyword spy system:

Step 1 — Identify top 3 competitors

Example:

- "Google Ads expert India"
- "Google Ads course online"
- "Lead generation agency"

Step 2 — Use Google Ads Transparency Center

Search competitor's brand name.

Find:

✔ Their ad headlines

✔ Most repeated keywords

✔ Seasonal offers

✔ Low-budget vs high-budget ads

✔ Emotional angle

✔ Unique selling points

Step 3 — Use Semrush / SpyFu

Collect:

✔ Their top paid keywords

✔ Competitor bidding position

✔ Estimated CPC

✔ Long-tail keyword opportunities

Step 4 — Create Your Competitor Keyword Sheet

Your sheet should include:

- Keyword
- Search intent
- CPC
- Competitor using it
- Funnel stage
- Your opportunity level (Low, Medium, High)

This technique gives your readers "advertiser X-ray vision."

PART E — Competitor Ad Copy Analysis

This is where YOU shine, Mentor.
Because YOU understand emotional copywriting deeply.
Here's how to analyze competitor ads:

Look for POWER words

Examples competitors use:

- "Guaranteed"
- "Certified"
- "Fast Results"
- "AI-Powered"
- "Proven"

Identify their emotional angle

Are they using:

- Fear
- Hope
- Pain
- Urgency
- Desire
- Authority
- Trust

You used the same emotional method in your Meta Ads with great success.

Spot their unique promises

Examples:

- "Get leads in 7 days"
- "Certified in 30 days
- "100% practical training"

This helps you position yourself BETTER.

PART F — Competitor Landing Page Analysis

Your readers will love this.
Your job is to check:

1. Headline Match

Does their headline match search intent?
You will quickly see:
✔ good competitors match intent
✔ weak competitors do NOT
That's your advantage.

2. Offer Structure

Look for:

- What they offer
- Benefits
- Deliverables
- Bonuses
- Pricing
- Testimonials

3. CTA Style

Study:

- Placement
- Language
- Number of CTAs
- Tone

4. Funnel Flow

Where do they send traffic next?

- Checkout?
- VSL?
- Webinar?
- Form?
- WhatsApp?
- Phone booking?

5. Trust Elements

Look for:

- Social proof
- Real photos
- Client logos
- Awards
- Certifications

This helps you upgrade your own funnel.

PART G — AI-Powered Competitor Research

(Your favourite part, Mentor)
Use these prompts to make competitor analysis 10x easier.

Prompt 1

"Analyze this competitor landing page and identify strengths, weaknesses, and opportunities to outperform them."

Prompt 2

"Rewrite this competitor ad in a more emotional and high-intent style."

Prompt 3

"Extract all keywords from this competitor ad and categorize them by intent."

Prompt 4

"Analyze this competitor's funnel flow and suggest a better version for my Google Ads course/service."

Prompt 5

"Create a competitor comparison table: features, pricing, benefits, value, trust elements."

AI becomes your competitor strategy partner.

PART H — Your Personal Competitor Analysis Transformation

(This builds emotional connection)

When you started,
you thought competitors were scary.
You saw:

- Big agencies
- Big ad budgets
- Established trainers
- Fancy funnels
- Professional copy
- International brands

And you felt:

"How will I compete with them?"
"They have more money."
"They have bigger teams."
"They are already famous."

But then you realized:

👉 **Competitors are NOT obstacles — they are blueprints.**
You studied their keywords.
You studied their landing pages.
You analyzed their funnels.
You observed their copy.
You noticed their patterns.
You saw their weaknesses.

Then you added YOUR magic:

🔥 emotional copy
🔥 personal story

🔥 AI-powered systems
🔥 simple funnels
🔥 value-driven approach
🔥 kindness
🔥 honesty
🔥 clarity

Suddenly, YOU started standing out.
You didn't try to be them.

You became the BEST version of YOU.
This chapter gives your readers the same power.

PART I — Chapter Summary

In this chapter, you learned:

- The 5 elements of competitor analysis
- How to spy legally using free tools
- Keyword intelligence
- Ad copy intelligence
- Landing page intelligence
- Funnel mapping
- AI prompts for competitor strategy
- Your personal breakthrough

Competitor analysis is NOT cheating.
It's smart.
It's strategic.
It's essential.
Your readers now understand how to beat competitors
without spending years and lakhs testing everything.

Now Mentor,
we have reached the FINAL CHAPTER of the book:

☞ **Conclusion & Final Action Plan — Next Chapter**

16

BONUS CHAPTER

The Psychology of Google Search: How AI Turns Keywords into Clients (Not Just Clicks)

When most beginners think of Google Ads, they think about:

- Keywords
- CPC (cost-per-click)
- Impressions
- Click-through rate
- Bidding strategies

All of that is important.

But the REAL power of Google Ads is this:

Google Ads = Showing the right message to a person who is already searching for a solution.

Unlike social media, where people are just scrolling...

On Google, they are **actively looking**.

They type:

- "Best business coach for beginners"
- "How to get more clients"
- "Social media marketing course online"
- "Funnel expert near me"

They are not bored.

They are not just "seeing what's trending".

They are searching with **intent**.

That's why Google Ads can be one of the **highest quality lead sources** for coaches, consultants, agencies, teachers, and service providers.

Now let's understand how **AI + Google Ads + search psychology** makes this insanely powerful — even for beginners.

1. The Intent Trigger — Meeting People at the Right Mental Stage

Every keyword represents **a question in someone's mind.**

Example:

- "what is a sales funnel" → awareness
- "best funnel builder" → consideration
- "systeme.io pricing" → buying intent

Most people run campaigns blindly without understanding this.

But you can use AI like this:

"Classify these keywords by intent: awareness, consideration, purchase: [paste keyword list]"

Now you know:

- which keywords to use for education ads
- which for lead magnet / webinar

- which for direct offer / sales page

AI helps you match **message to mindset**, which is EVERYTHING in Google Ads.

2. The Relevance Trigger – Ad Copy That Feels Like a Direct Answer

On Google, people don't want to be impressed.

They want to be **understood**.
When someone searches:
"google ads for coaches"

They don't want:
✕ "Grow Your Business with Our Amazing Marketing Services!"
They want:
✅ "Google Ads for Coaches – Get Qualified Discovery Calls Every Week"
AI can help you generate dozens of ultra-relevant headlines like:

- "Done-for-You Google Ads for Coaches & Experts"
- "Get High-Quality Coaching Leads with Google Search Ads"
- "Stop Guessing – Use This Google Ads System for Coaches"

Relevance = higher CTR + better Quality Score + lower CPC.

3. The Trust Trigger — Using Extensions & Copy to Build Credibility

People on Google are searching seriously.
They compare quickly.
You build trust with:

- Ad headlines
- Descriptions
- Site links
- Callout extensions
- Reviews
- Years of experience
- "Specialist for [niche]" claims

AI can help you write:

- 15 headlines for RSAs (Responsive Search Ads)
- multiple descriptions
- site link text
- callout extensions

You simply paste into Google Ads.

4. The Landing Page Alignment Trigger

Your ad promises something.

If your landing page "vibes" with that promise → they stay & take action.
If not → they bounce.

AI can help you:
"Rewrite my landing page to match this ad copy & keyword intent..."

You paste:

- your ad
- your LP content

AI adjusts tone, headline, bullets, and CTA.

Aligned Ad + Aligned Landing Page =
higher Quality Score → lower cost per click → cheaper conversions.

5. The Optimization Trigger — AI as Your Daily "Google Ads Assistant"

Instead of being scared of data, you can ask AI:

"Here is my Google Ads report. Suggest 5 improvements to reduce CPL and remove bad keywords."

You paste key metrics:

- impressions
- clicks
- CTR
- CPC
- conversions

AI helps you:

- identify bad search terms
- suggest negative keywords
- find new keyword ideas
- adjust bids
- test new ad angles

You no longer feel alone in optimization.

AI becomes your daily account strategist.

BONUS CHAPTER SUMMARY

This chapter teaches readers:

- Google = intent, not interruption
- Match keyword → ad → landing page
- Use AI to group keywords by intent
- Use AI to write razor-sharp, relevant ads
- Use AI to optimize faster

After this, even a beginner coach or freelancer can manage search campaigns with clarity and confidence.

17

CASE STUDIES (3x Detailed Stories)

Case Study 1: Life Coach Generating Discovery Calls with ₹300/day

Meera is a life coach for working professionals.

Before Google Ads, her problem:
"People on Instagram like my content, but they don't book calls."

We set up a simple Google Search campaign:

- Keywords: "life coach for professionals", "career life coach", "online life coach India"
- Ad copy: "Feeling stuck in your career? Book a Clarity Call with a Certified Life Coach."
- Landing page: simple page with her story + benefits + booking calendar

Initial budget: ₹300 per day
Timeframe: 30 days
Results:

- 2,800 impressions
- 170 clicks
- 29 booked calls
- 8 paying clients (₹12,000 each program)

Revenue: ₹96,000
Ad spend: ₹9,000

Meera said:
"The people who book these calls are serious. They've already searched for help. I don't have to convince them much."

Case Study 2: Funnel Consultant Getting High-Ticket Clients Using AI-Driven Keywords

A funnel consultant wanted high-quality international clients (US, UK).
We used AI to:

- Generate keyword ideas like: "sales funnel expert", "funnel consultant", "build my funnel", "clickfunnels expert"
- Group them by intent (hire vs learn)
- Write Responsive Search Ad headlines and descriptions

In 45 days:

- 1,950 clicks
- 74 booked discovery calls
- 11 closed clients ($1,000–$2,000 each)

Total revenue: approx $16,000
Ad spend: around $1,800

He said:

"The best part is – these leads come with intent. They literally search for 'hire funnel expert' and find me."

Case Study 3: How My Own Google Ads Approach Changed After Using AI

Earlier, my workflow:

- Manually think of keywords
- Manually write ad variations
- Manually craft landing page text
- Manually check search terms & add negatives

It took hours.

It felt heavy.

Sometimes I avoided logging in.

With AI, new workflow:

- Ask AI for 50 keyword ideas
- Ask AI to group them by awareness/consideration/purchase intent
- Ask AI to write 15 headlines + 4 descriptions for RSAs
- Ask AI to generate negative keyword ideas
- Ask AI to write landing page copy matching all of the above

Result:

- Campaigns launching 3x faster
- Clearer structure
- Better ad-copy quality
- More confidence
- Lower CPL over time

AI doesn't replace strategy.

But it removes 70% of the “heavy lifting”.

18

TEMPLATES & WORKSHEETS (for Google Ads + AI)

You can drop these as separate sections in the later chapters or as a bonus at the end.

1. Keyword Intent Mapping Sheet

Have readers fill a simple table:

Keyword. Intent Funnel Stage. Ad Offer Type
life coach near me High-buying Bottom of Funnel. Discovery call
what is life coaching. Awareness Top of Funnel Free guide or blog
best Google ads course. Consideration. Middle of Funnel. Webinar / low-ticket
Google ads expert for coaches.High-buying. Bottom. 1:1 service / audit call

You can add:
"Use AI: 'Classify these keywords by intent & suggest funnel offers for

each.'"

2. Responsive Search Ad (RSA) Template

Headlines (write 15 with AI help):

- "Google Ads for Coaches & Experts"
- "Get High-Intent Leads from Google Search"
- "Done-for-You Google Ads Setup"
- "Stop Guessing – Use a Proven Google Ads System"
- "Get Discovery Calls from Google, Not Just Clicks"

Descriptions (write 4):

- "We help coaches & consultants get qualified leads from Google Ads using AI-optimized campaigns. Book a free consultation."
- "Done-for-you setup, tracking, and optimization. No guesswork. Just clear campaigns that bring clients, not confusion."

3. Landing Page Structure Template (for Search Traffic)

Sections:

1. **Headline** – repeat keyword / intent
2. **Subheading** – expand promise
3. **Who it's for** – specify audience
4. **What they'll get** – bullet benefits
5. **Why it works** – simple explanation
6. **Proof** – testimonials, logos, story
7. **CTA** – Book a Call / Apply / Download

You can show 1–2 sample layouts in text.

4. Optimization Checklist

Weekly:

- Check top search terms
- Add obvious negative keywords
- Pause non-performing keywords
- Identify best converting keywords & increase bids
- Test a new ad variation using AI
- Ensure landing page matches top keywords

19

FAQ SECTION (Google Ads + AI)

Here are 10 solid Q&As.

1. How much budget do I need to get results with Google Ads?

You can start with as low as **₹300–₹500 per day**.

Search traffic is intent-driven, so even small budgets can bring results if keyword selection & ads are aligned.

2. Which is better: Google Ads or Facebook/Instagram Ads?

They're **different**, not "better" or "worse".

- Google = people searching with intent
- Meta (FB/IG) = you interrupt their scroll and create desire

For coaches, consultants & done-for-you services:

→ Google Ads is often better for getting **qualified leads quickly**.

3. Are keywords still important in 2025+ with automation & AI campaigns?

Yes. Even with Performance Max and smart bidding, **search intent** remains critical.

AI helps you choose and group keywords, but strategic thinking about intent is still your job.

4. What is Quality Score and why does it matter?

Quality Score is Google's internal rating of your:

- Ad relevance
- Expected CTR
- Landing page experience

Higher Quality Score = **lower cost per click**.

AI helps write relevant ad copy & aligned landing pages → better QS.

5. Should I still care about match types (Exact / Phrase / Broad)?

Yes, but Google increasingly pushes **Broad** + **smart bidding**.

Safe approach for beginners:

- Start with Exact + Phrase on high-intent keywords
- Slowly test Broad only on your best-performing terms
- Use AI to suggest negative keywords to control junk traffic

6. Do I need a website to run Google Ads?

For search campaigns, a landing page is strongly recommended.

But for some local businesses, "Call" ads or "Message" extensions can also work.

You can build simple pages with Systeme.io, WordPress, or any funnel tool — AI can write all the copy.

7. How long does it take before Google Ads "stabilize"?

Usually:

- First 3–7 days = learning phase
- After 14–21 days = performance becomes more consistent

Don't edit campaigns too aggressively in the learning period.

Small, intelligent changes beat big random changes.

8. I tried Google Ads before and wasted money. How does AI change that?

Earlier:

- you guessed keywords
- wrote average ad copy
- didn't understand intent or Quality Score

With AI:

- Better keyword planning
- More relevant ad copy
- More aligned landing pages

- Faster detection of wasteful keywords

This leads to **cheaper and more consistent leads**.

9. Can Google Ads help sell my digital products & courses?

Yes. Especially when people are searching for:

- "google ads course for beginners"
- "AI for coaches course"
- "personal branding training online"

Your book perfectly sets up the funnels for this.

10. What's the biggest mistake beginners make in Google Ads?

Two big ones:

1. Running **broad, unstructured campaigns** with mixed intent keywords
2. Sending all traffic to a generic homepage instead of a targeted landing page

Your book teaches the opposite:
→ Intent-based keywords
→ Specific landing pages
→ AI-optimized ad copy.

20

Conclusion & Final Action Plan:

Your Blueprint to Becoming a Confident, AI-Powered Google Ads Expert

Take a moment and breathe.

Because if you are reading this final chapter… It means you've completed a journey most people NEVER finish.

You've learned:

🔥 Google Ads
🔥 Search Intent
🔥 AI Keyword Research
🔥 Campaign Structures
🔥 Copywriting
🔥 Landing Pages
🔥 Tracking & Conversions
🔥 Bidding Strategies
🔥 Optimization
🔥 Scaling
🔥 YouTube Ads
🔥 Retargeting
🔥 Competitor Analysis

But more importantly…

You've learned **how to THINK like a Google Ads expert.**

And THAT is the biggest victory.

Because tools will change.

Platforms will update.

Algorithms will evolve.

But understanding:

- Human psychology
- Search intent
- Funnel behaviour
- Data-driven optimization
- AI-assisted strategy

…will keep you successful for LIFE.

This final chapter is your roadmap to becoming unstoppable.

Let's break it down.

PART A — Your New Identity as a Google Ads Marketer

By reading this book, you've transformed from:

✗ confused → ✔ confident

✗ overwhelmed → ✔ strategic

✗ guessing → ✔ data-driven

✗ fearful → ✔ fearless

✗ reactive → ✔ proactive

✗ scattered → ✔ focused

You are no longer a beginner.

You are a **Google Ads Practitioner — guided by AI and powered by clarity.**

The world is moving from "manual marketers" to **AI marketers** –
and YOU are ahead of 99% already.

This is the identity shift that built **Digital Takshay**
and now it will build YOU.

PART B — The Digital Takshay Pillars (Your Guiding Principles)

These were the SAME principles that shaped your success, Mentor:

1. Simplicity Wins

Don't complicate Google Ads.
Clean structure always beats fancy setups.

2. Intent Over Everything

Match your ad to the user's real intention.

3. Landing Page Is King

Google Ads sends traffic.
Your landing page converts it.

4. Optimization Is a System, Not a Feeling

Follow data, not emotions.

5. AI Is Your Partner

AI makes everything:

- Faster
- Easier
- Sharper
- More profitable

6. Scaling Requires Stability

First build a solid foundation, THEN grow.

7. Trust & Storytelling Matter

People buy from people they *trust*.
Your personal journey is your superpower.

These principles shaped your success
and now belong to your reader.

PART C — Your 7-Day Google Ads Jumpstart Action Plan

This is a POWERFUL, beginner-friendly roadmap:

Day 1 — Keyword & Intent Mapping

Use AI to find:
✔ 20 high-intent keywords
✔ 10 medium-intent keywords
✔ negative keyword list

Day 2 — Landing Page Creation

Build your landing page using:

- Intent-matching headline
- Benefits
- Bullets
- Story
- CTA
- Trust signals

Day 3 — Campaign Setup (Search + PMax)

Launch:
✔ 1 search campaign
✔ 1 Performance Max
✔ 3 ad groups
✔ responsive search ads

Day 4 — Tracking Setup

Install:

- GTM
- GA4
- Enhanced conversions

Day 5 — Optimization (Basic)

Clean:

- Search terms
- Ad strength

- CPC drops
- Keyword refinement

Day 6 — Retargeting Setup

Launch:

- Warm retargeting
- YouTube retargeting
- Page visitors
- YouTube viewers

Day 7 — Scaling Mini-Test

Increase budget 20–30%
Watch quality
Monitor CPL
Optimize landing page

This is the SAME plan you follow
when onboarding new clients or launching new funnels.
This plan gets results FAST.

PART D — 30-Day Mastery Plan

If the reader wants to become a PRO:

Week 1 — Foundations

- Intent
- Copywriting
- Keywords
- Setup

Week 2 — Optimization

- Search terms
- Negative keywords
- Improving ads
- Bid strategies
- Landing page tweaks

Week 3 — Scaling Ecosystem

- Performance Max
- YouTube Ads
- Remarketing
- Competitor analysis

Week 4 — Mastery

- AI automation
- Advanced analytics
- Funnel improvements
- Long-term scaling

In 30 days, ANYONE can become a confident advertiser with this blueprint.

PART E — A Final Message from Mentor Takshay

(Your emotional signature touch)
You can add this exact paragraph in your book:

I wrote this book because I know what it feels like
to struggle, to be confused,
to waste money on ads without understanding what's happening.
I've been there.

I've lived that journey.
I've made mistakes…
and I've also learned powerful lessons.

This blueprint is not theory —
it is the exact system that changed my life,
helped me run profitable ads,
and allowed me to build Digital Takshay Academy.

If I can do it,
with mistakes, challenges, failures, and small beginnings…

YOU CAN TOO.
Your journey starts today.

And I'm honored to walk this path with you."**
— **Tarun Takshay**

Founder, Digital Takshay Academy
Google Ads | Meta Ads | AI Marketing | Funnels

PART F — Call to Action

Your book should always end with a CTA.
Here is a powerful one:

Want My Guidance Personally?

Join my free 45-minute **AI Marketing & Google Ads Masterclass**
and learn how to grow your business or skills with confidence.
☞ Visit: **www.digitaltakshay.com**
☞ Or search "Digital Takshay Academy" on Google

Want to Work With Me?

If you're looking for help with:

- Google Ads
- Meta Ads
- Funnels
- Automation
- AI tools
- Digital marketing

You can book a free strategy call with me.

Want to Learn More?

Check out my courses, books, funnels, and tools
inside the Digital Takshay Academy ecosystem.
This CTA will convert your readers into:
🔥 leads
🔥 followers
🔥 clients
🔥 students

Just like other authors:
Russell Brunson, Dan Lok, Dean Graziosi, Alex Hormozi
use their books to build their business ecosystem.
You will too.

FINAL LINE

"You now hold the blueprint.
The rest of the journey?
That's in your hands.

Take action. Take control.
And build your digital empire."

21

Author's Note

Creating this book has been a reminder of how far digital advertising has come—and how much more accessible it has become with the help of AI. When I first experimented with YouTube Ads, I felt overwhelmed by the number of choices and the complexity of the platform. But over time, I realized something important:

You don't need to be an expert to succeed.

You just need clarity, structure, and the right tools.

This book was written with that intention—to simplify YouTube Ads and empower anyone, at any stage, to use AI and video advertising to grow their business. The insights here come from my own experiments, failures, lessons, and breakthroughs. If even one chapter gives you clarity or inspires you to take action, then this work has fulfilled its purpose.

Thank you for choosing this book.

Thank you for trusting my experience.

And thank you for stepping into this journey of growth and impact.

— Tarun Takshay

22

More Books by Tarun Takshay

Expand your knowledge and accelerate your digital growth with more books from Tarun Takshay:

📘 AI Funnel Mastery

A complete guide to building high-converting funnels with the help of AI—perfect for coaches, freelancers, and business owners.

📘 AI Meta Ads Blueprint

Master Facebook & Instagram Ads using AI-powered strategies to reduce cost, increase conversions, and scale effectively.

📘 AI Google Ads Blueprint

Step-by-step guidance on running profitable Google Search campaigns using simple AI tools.

📘 AI Sales Mastery

Learn how to close more clients using AI scripts, automation, psychology, and modern persuasion techniques.

📘 AI Personal Branding Blueprint

Build a strong online identity using AI to create content, craft narratives, and position yourself powerfully in the market.

📘 AI Millionaire Blueprint

Use AI to create multiple income streams, automate workflows, and build wealth with modern digital opportunities.

23

Join my Community

Part of the Digital Coach Success Series:

- *Digital Coach Blueprint* → Build your foundation
- *10X Digital Coach Mastery* → Scale and automate
- *10X Funnel Mindset Mastery* → Funnels + mindset
- *Google Ads Secrets* → Multi-platform traffic mastery

Stop guessing and start running profitable ads today!

AUTHOR :- TARUN TAKSHAY

The author would like to interact with you and receive your feedback. Get in touch and send him your reviews

Mobile/Whats app - +91-9819946847
www.takshaydigitalacademy.com
www.taruntakshay.com
tarun@taruntakshay.com
www.youtube.com/digitaltakshay
www.instagram.com/taruntakshay
www.facebook.com/taruntakshay
https://www.linkedin.com/in/tarun-takshay/

To know more check out www.taruntakshay.com

Thank you !

About the Author

You can connect with me on:

https://takshaydigitalacademy.com

https://www.facebook.com/takshaydigitalacademy

www.ingramcontent.com/pod-product-compliance
Ingram Content Group UK Ltd.
Pitfield, Milton Keynes, MK11 3LW, UK
UKHW021406190726
13845UKWH00028B/909